Journey Through Willowseyez

Book One

Rev. Katherine Christensen

Journey Through Willowseyez. Copyright © 2007 by Katherine Christensen. All rights reserved. No part of this book may be used or reproduced in any manner whatsoever, including Internet usage, without written permission of the publisher except in the case of brief quotations embodied in critical articles and reviews.

First Edition

Cover design: © Katherine M. Christensen

  1.Christianity----2. Wicca----3. Spiritualism Metaphysics----Healing

ISBN   978-0-6151-5623-1

Dedication

This book is dedicated to everyone I love, to every influential family members, friends, and teachers throughout my life who shared their knowledge.
Most of all, the beautiful whispering in my ears combined with the gift of inside sight from the Divine Source guiding me to write this book!

With
Love from me to you!

PREFACE

This book is for those who want to connect to the Divine Source, but finds it difficult in doing so. I'll try to help through with structure and consistency. I feel everyone should experience what I know; it is so satisfying and it would be selfish if I held back information that would help others connect with the Divine Source. It took most of my life to reach this point to where I could gather such great information and place it all together in a book. I believe this book will help answer your questions, learn facts, and do what is correct and for the good of all! I would like to express my gratitude to everyone who made fundamental and frequent contributions of information, leading to ideas of the overall style of this book. I found enormous delight gathering information while on my life journey while maintaining higher principals to gain rewards captured throughout this book. Many heartfelt thanks to all and your suggestions.

By
Reverend Katherine Christensen

ABOUT THE AUTHOR

I was born into the armed forces in Chandler Arizona, the 21st of April, 1959. My personality was very much misunderstood by family members as a child because they thought I was too much under the influence of a military structure. They would call me miss prissy because my family felt I knew too much and I couldn't tolerate wrong doings from my siblings or my parents. At a very early age I had a strong sense of what was right and wrong. It wasn't from the military's influence but my close connection to the Divine Source. I never felt like I fit in to this particular family because each family member had extreme negative traits. It was very frightening to be born within a dark circle of people. I guess this was my first test in this life to know, recognize, and escape while maintaining my closeness to the Divine. Yes, sadly I do have to admit, my parents were just the vehicle to get me here. I can't find any other reason I would be born into such an unloving family. However, I do love them for giving me life; to start me on my path, even if it was a shock to see such darkness radiating around me daily. There are days I do have to remember that when we ask to be born, to our parents they do have to agree. In the center of that dark circle there must have been some light, but where is it? Only the Divine Source knows how many times I've tried to convince my family that there is so much more out there for them, but their negativity would get in the way, or push me away. I do believe both parents had some sort of psychological disorders, father with either severe depression or A.D.D., and mother with O.C.D. of over spending and neglecting her home financial responsibilities, if I had a PH.D in psychology, this would be what I would have diagnosed. Both of these disorders hurt my further growth dramatically. Back in the day people were shunned if there were any traits of psychological disorders and were called mental then sent to institutions for life. These cases were hush hush or denied. Many children suffered because of the lack of appropriate medication and therapy was not administered to parents; therefore many children lived what they learned so I do forgive you mom and dad for you were just as frightened as I was, but now its time to get with the program. This era was difficult for both parents and children, how can you expect these children to excel through this frightening experience? For me, it was grade school that saved my life. Teachers knew parents were under educated, frightened and confused. They knew my potential, took me under their wing and guided me correctly on my path. They gave me a little more attention when needed. I am grateful for laws that forced children to go to school because I can honestly say it saved my life. The same time we began school, my parents insisted their children had to go to church and Sunday school. Not for the reason of learning about the Divine Source, but for the reason they wanted quiet time on Sunday mornings. I rebelled feeling forced within this religion. I went anyway because I did enjoy the stories of the Old Testament. Although their judgmental God they portrayed frightened me so. I knew he was pure Love and that is all. They didn't need to frighten mankind or more so the children, just to get their point across through manipulating conformity Their thought was to use scare tactics so the parishioners would be too fearful to leave. It is actually backfiring upon them and people are running from this religion. I found this religion to be very strict, stifling, and unloving. Another rule they enforced was; thou shall not bow down to statues (idols) in other religions, what about the statues in their own religion. In all religions, they have statues, but this is how they perceive the Divine, they all believe in the Divine as we do. They just see him differently. The fact is there is but one Divine Source, no matter how you think he looks. The Christian religion has so much fear within; it was this fear that drove me away. Their excuses of their perception of natural laws drove me to an urgency to seek the Divine Light and Love that I knew really existed. For all the wonders of the world the Christians would label these wonders as non existence or demonic characters, which in fact everything is made from the Divine, everything is! These contradictions are an insult to my intelligence at an early age. One day I left this religion, never to return. I quit church, school and ran away from home, not to be a quitter, but to find my correct path. I did, however learn the origin of the Divine and the step by step guide from Genesis to

Revelations and wanted to follow this Divine Spirit as did the twelve Disciples. It was difficult for a few years, living in different homes with friends, never feeling comfortable or at total peace, just trying to fit in, but didn't wish to return back to my earlier life just yet. I did manage to finish school and start college while away from home, so it wasn't all bad. At the age of eighteen, I married; shortly after the marriage I was pregnant with my first child. Because of the way I was raised my experience as a mom wasn't the greatest with my first born. I too didn't show a lot of love, which caused a dysfunctional relationship with this child, even today, this relationship is distant. Hopefully she will read this and forgive me as I did with my parents. I didn't stop at one child I had three more and vowed to myself I would show them all the love in the world. These relationships are very close and loving. Another lesson learned the lesson of unconditional love. Shortly after the births I divorced because I too loved myself enough to get out of yet, another dark circle. I wasn't allowed to work, drive a car, and make phone calls, just pregnant and barefoot. With my strong will, I again threw my hands up and took my life back, walking, excuse me running away from this situation. While in this marriage, my life was at a standstill, a cement figurine, I chipped away daily at the center of this cement casting to set myself free once again. A few years after the divorce I met this gentleman Paul, He was tall dark and definitely handsome, I totally love him, and still do to this day! He was a lot of fun, even with his recreational drug use. I partnered with him for a few years until I noticed that his recreational drug use became an addictive issue that was not appropriate behavior around my children. I had to let him go, which broke my heart. My children needed a parent who will teach them the correct way through life and to keep them protected. Of course, I chose my children, but I will always love Paul. By leaving I was forced to maintain three jobs to keep my family afloat. I worked as a Certified Nurses Aide, managed the service desk at the local Ames department store, and worked weekends cleaning hotel rooms. This went on until my last child graduated high school. The lesson learned at this point was selflessness (giving of you without expecting anything in return). Now that my mind is free from my parenting responsibility I was able to give thought as to what my life purpose was. I had a lot of questions, who am I, why am I here, what am I suppose to do, and how am I going to get there? I knew I was already walking the correct path even through all trials and errors that life threw at me, and continued maintaining a closeness to the Divine. Now I want to become one with the Divine. At the turn of the Millennium, my life had changed suddenly and irrevocably within a single period of twenty-four hours. I began to work on this book through journals, not with any intent of publishing it, but rather, out of necessity. Family and friends thought they met a new person, and wondered where the old Katherine went. I found I didn't recognize myself either. Without warning or acceptance on my part, psychic phenomena occurred in my life on a daily basis. They included everything you read or watch on television, the E.S.P., seeing auras, communication with spirits or higher intelligences, channeling, psychic healing, all this was happening to me. I managed to keep my sanity within journals; the more I worked with the techniques in my journals, the more spiritually advanced I became. In 2004 I remarried to a gentleman, Jeffery that was finally on the same spiritual level as I am, honestly, he is slightly more advanced than I. Through his love, he encourages me to follow my dreams. He refuses to allow my mind to become lazy, he can be quite harsh at times, but I do know it is for my own good and for the good of all. I appreciate his encouragement, the more encouragement he shows the more I grow. I know he is very proud of my development, he speaks of it daily. I can honestly say he has helped the most in my spiritual advancement. And I thank and love him for that. Within this book I will show you how I became one with the Divine. We all have our ups and downs in life; the object of the game of life is to keep afloat with a positive attitude, canceling ego, growth in self structure, and applying consistency. I continue to overcome life lessons; it will be this way until I go home to the Other Side. So cheer up, you're not alone in this game of life, my life purpose is to help you on your way. Also my book is far from perfect; it is written this way because I want you to deal with these frustrations positively, so I've inadvertently made mistakes within. I'm not perfect, far from it, and admit I still have a lot to learn, so I created this book as far down to earth as possible with natural human error. This book is very legible; the mistakes are minor and barely noticeable. The key is not to pick away at the mistakes within, but read and absorb what's within. Just chuckle, move on, and continue to read about whom, why where, when, how and what you want to become.

TABLE OF CONTENTS

Chapter I
Introduction and Christian Beliefs……………………………………………………*1 - 20*
Journal……………………………………………………………*Back of each page*

Chapter II
Wicca Beliefs………………………………………………………………*21 – 54*

Chapter III
Tarot and Spreads………………………………………………………...*55 - 82*

Chapter IV
Karma Debt and Astrology……………………………………………….....*83 - 132*

Chapter V
Psychometry, Dreams, and pendulum………………………………………....*133- 158*

Chapter VI
My Book of Shadows, Contemplation and Spells……………………………*159 - 290*

Chapter VII
Mediumship, all you should know………………………………………*291 – 418*

Chapter VIII
Basic Healing………………………………………………………………......*419 - 461*

CHAPTER I
INTRODUCTION

I will be speaking briefly about Christianity, its pros and cons, elaborate a little more about Wicca Religion and onto Spiritualism, it was here within these two religions where I came to realize there was so much more to life and love than that of the Christian religion. I will try not to be too judgmental toward any religion, I will simply describe in my opinion what I had actually learned and concluded within these mentioned This is my path, yours may differ, and hopefully the ending result will be the same. There is much we have to learn, we don't and can not possibly know everything, and all you can do is to advance spiritually within your own individual growth. At the end of our spiritual journey we should end in the same place, side by side next to the Divine. I've also included a journal within so you can compare my theories; write your thoughts, or just remember something within. You have to remember we are all born with a psychic gift, they are meant to assist while in our physical bodies to maintain our spiritual awareness and connection to the Divine. For every physical sense these is a psychic sense that corresponds with it. For example, Have you ever made a phone call, went to pick up the phone to dial and the person you were calling was already on the other end? Well here's the good news; you're not crazy. These incidents happen all the time but we tend to ignore them, due to the fact that we're born into a society of multiple religions, science, and technology that has moved us away from our own inner knowing or your psychic abilities. Freedom is not freedom over others or freedom from others but freedom from your own boundaries, the limits and conditions into which you have thrown yourself.

NOTES

We have access to fresh, yet timeless guidance for the art of living, living awake, living lovingly, and living in the light of the Divine. So, in order to transform others, you first have to transform yourself. How are we, as individuals, to understand our responsibilities toward Mother Earth in this critical time? What is our most immediate issue? To save the rain forests, use less water, stop factories from polluting the four essential elements? We can't even come close in conquering any of these single handedly. First if we are to start the real process of world change, we must begin with ourselves. Within this book, I will help you discover your own psychic abilities through various exercises that will break down the learning process. And to allow you not to get caught up in the dogma of any religion, just be religious and stay close to spirit. If you feel trapped into anything just <u>run</u> so to stay on your own path, never try to appease everyone. It's all about what's right for you. It's your path and on one else's. Not what anyone demands what is right for you! I don't like to dispute this religion but the illustration below shows exactly how I felt. I am neither a zombie nor a puppet that needs to be misdirected throughout my entire life. This phases of my spiritual journey was my introduction to spirit, I was just disappointed in the way this religion portrayed him.

NOTES

CHRISTIANITY
THE TEN COMMANDMENTS

1. *I am the Lord your God. Thou shall have no other Gods before me.*
2. *Thou shall not make yourself a God in any form from Heaven, Earth, or waters. Thou shall not bow down to them or worship them. For I am a jealous God, and will punish the children for their fathers sins now and in the third and fourth generation of those who hate me, but showing love to a thousand generations of those who love me and keep my commandments.*
3. *Thou shall not take thy Lord's name in vain.*
4. *Thou shall observe the Sabbath day, the seventh day ye shall rest.*
5. *Honor thy Mother and thy Father.*
6. *Thou shall not kill.*
7. *Thou shall not commit adultery.*
8. *Thou shall not steal.*
9. *Thou shall not desire thy neighbors' wife.*
10. *Thou shall not desire thy neighbor's possessions.*

NOTES

Bethlehem or Nazareth, the cradle of Christianity, where Emperor Tiberius Caesar tried to acclimate Christianity from the Pagan Religion. Today a lot of the Pagan Religion still exist. Within many churches they light candles, light the frankincense, chant, weather it be the rosary or other chants. Churches are almost always dimly lit; all these techniques were of the Pagan religion before Christianity. In all religions you feel a definite touch of spirit. No church is better than the next, as long as man has a place to pray. I left Christianity because there were too many excuses made against the natural laws, too political, way too judgmental, consisting of reprogramming our brains for their cultural conditioning; sort of a brainwashing. Don't misunderstand me I did have some great memories within this religion, but their negativity weighed out the positive aspects on how they wanted to have a grand following. I will in brief give you some examples where Christianity would evade the natural laws. I make no attempt to discredit this religion or to persuade you in any way to change your path. These are merely my opinions and conclusions. The Incarnation of Jesus Christ was actually the Divine Source himself, to correct the remnant of the fall leading to much evil by mankind's freewill.

<u>*Materialization and Teleporting*</u>

The question is asked, can a person be at two places at the same time? Back in the nineteenth century, in Mexico, a class of students witnessed their teacher standing and writing on the chalk board when her double appeared beside her. On a second occasion, it was clearly visible that this teacher was outside walking through a garden toward the school when the same teacher materialized within the classroom. The students were in awe and disbelief that two students touched the apparition. They said it felt like muslin; another student walked boldly through her. This was enough evidence for them, and how could thirty students tell the same story with no truth to it. Christianity's statement for this was it was a fanciful elaboration.

NOTES

Telepathy is the explanation, sometimes apparitions can be projected telepathically into the minds of others, and then their minds stimulate and produce a recognizable image. This image will act naturally and usually obey physical laws such as producing reflection within a mirror or communicating verbally.

<u>Black Holes</u>

Black holes are formed by a star that burns up all its internal energy and collapses inward leaving a stronger and stronger gravitational pull until it becomes infinitely small. It soaks up all light not allowing any to escape, becoming invisible. It sucks in nearby objects into itself, crushing it. Inside its event horizon, time operates differently. Some scientists suggest that travelers drawn into this hole will emerge on the other side into another dimension. This is one theory Christianity can not bash. Unfortunately these holes do exist.

<u>Yoga</u>

This is a spiritual discipline by which man reaches union with the Divine Source. One branch is hatha yoga, involving physical posture exercise to achieve psychic power and to prepare the mind for spiritual enlightenment. Christianity believes that yoga can be helpful but because of the Hindu roots they fear their occult involvement.

<u>Fire Walking</u>

Some psychic researchers undertook fire-walking experiments in 1935, and concluded the secret was that each foot touched the embers for less than a half a second, not long enough to burn. In Hindu these fire-walkers have been slow dignified affairs. The true explanation is most fire-walkers slip into a trance state which induces a natural anesthesia. Participants prepare themselves spiritually before hand, and are unharmed by their slow barefooted walk over the hot embers. In Christianity, this phenomenon is considered demon possession, an evil degree of spirit influence.

~~~~~~~~~~NOTES~~~~~~~~~~~~~

Mental Mysteries

Our bodies and minds possess powers which we have not yet learned to use. It is right that we should explore our potential to the full. By doing so we will find answers we are looking for and even find personal fulfillment we desire. We were made in the image of the Divine Source and made good, hence it is important to realize that exploring the nature of man will bring us face to face not only to our full potential but a closeness to the Divine Source. Christianity has induced such fear in man causing man to rebel against their creator, even causing man to fall from the light. The bible teaches because of sin Infinite is "outside" our lives this sort of condemnation blocks man from their relationship with the Divine Source and man's true human nature.

Seeing the Future

Planets have a Hugh influence in our lives causing astrology to advice man. These stars can even affect a person's choice in careers. Astrology began when man noticed the sun moving around the earth in a regular yearly path, spending an unknown length of time in the vicinity of each twelve group of stars. These star constellations divided the heavens into your twelve houses. Your destiny is then dictated by which house the sun is in and which planet were in the same house when you were born. This is why it is so crucial to know your exact time of birth because the date is not enough. In a more spiritually advanced society, we now realize that astrology may not be as accurate as other techniques because of the natural laws that govern the universe. These planets are supposed to influence our lives, except for Neptune and Pluto, which are ignored, they had not been discovered when the astrology rules were formed. There is also a thirteenth constellation, Ophiucus that is also never mentioned.

NOTES

Also you have to remember that the sun does not spend an equal amount of time in each house; an accurate example would be while sun stays six days in Scorpio it surpasses and stays a grand of forty-seven days in Virgo. These constellations are not real group of stars; they only appear to be when viewed from earth. The fact is two stars in the Orion Belt are closer to earth then they are to their partner stars in the constellation. Over the years, the heaven has shifted, so in actuality, someone born in early October is considered a Libra, but a quick look into your telescope will in fact prove they are actually in Scorpio. Tarot cards contain pictures with various occult meanings, and when laid out in a certain order they will read out a message for you about the future. These forms of divinity are devices or tools to tell clients things they already subconsciously know. Crystal ball gazing is a form of automatism in which the subconscious mind sends messages in picture form to the conscious self. Clairvoyants, mediums, and sensitives; these tools were provided to us through the Divine Source. Today society is recognizing man's abilities protecting and justifying them through "premonitions bureaux", the first two located in San Francisco, CA. These places are made available for members of the public can report their premonitions of future disasters. An American mathematician surveyed severe train and plane crashes over several years and calculated that whenever there was a crash there were invariably fewer people in it than might have been expected. When a crash was coming, intuitively people would either change their bookings, decide not to travel, or choose an alternate route. This phenomenon is "life's receptivity to very subtle stimuli that tells you that the future has already started", our natural animal instinct to danger where our precognition exists. It's not difficult to see why we want to know the future in this uncertain world we live in. The rate of change is constantly moving forward to future shock exposing us to unpleasant surprises. These tools are given to us to use for our security and a feeling of being forewarned.

NOTES

Christianity says these tools represent a bizarre attempt to fuse their reliable methods with these uncommonly unreliable sources of data. It is better if man knows nothing for revelations of the future and is quite useless and irrelevant. Remember Christianity has their book of revelations of foreseeing the future.

<u>*Jinxes and Curses*</u>

Curses can be placed on other people by methods such as spells, sticking pins into wax images and reciting incantations. The intense concentration involved can bring psychic power to bear on the victim's mind. Often in a primitive tribe, a man who knows or feels they have been cursed will simply lie down and die, not because of the curse, but they are convinced they will die anyway. Some stories suggest active malice by a real, personal disincarnated entity. Certainly the power of curses is unpredictable and dangerous; those who try to capture it usually find that it has captured them. Christian would recognize this as an evil spirit, I do as well. Christians also believe that the powers of evil have been conquered by Christ's death, and that this victory over evil can be exercised by only Christians today. A great example for this is the graffiti you see on buildings all over the world in any city or suburbs. Gangs sending negative energy to other gangs. Whether positive or negative thinking, it will be sent out. Just remember what you send always returns to you more severe. So always think positive thoughts and you'll always receive positive returns.

<u>*The Life Beyond*</u>

Christianity's teachings about life after death conflicts profoundly with the information about the other side, usually offered by spirits. Witnessing reports given by the deceased son of Bishop James Pike. The Bishop's son states I haven't heard anything personally about Jesus. Nobody around here seems to talk about him. When we come over here, we have a choice, to remain as we are, or to grow in our understanding. Some still seem to be church minded and are waiting for a Judgment Day, they seem to be the unenlightened ones.

NOTES

Christianity's belief is in heaven there shall no more be anything accursed (deserving to be cursed or damned), but the throne of God and of the Lamb (Jesus) shall be in it, and his servants shall worship him; and they shall see his face. It is appointed for men to die once and after that comes judgment. They had a real difficult time giving appraisals or incentives instead they gave rule after rule, to where it is near impossible for mankind to be with the Divine Source unless you're a Priest, Minister, or any clergyman. Their belief is that once you go to heaven you stay there. We are of the same spirit as the Divine as was Jesus which was resurrected. Was he really dead or just in a coma? And why is just Christianity allowed to speak to spirit and not society?

Stigmata

These are real wounds, corresponding to the wounds of Christ, which magically appear on an individual's forehead, wrists and feet. Stigmata have appeared sporadically in church history since the thirteenth century, and several cases have been recorded this century. The Christians manifested a healthy skepticism toward stigmatic; they even disowned parishioners even after they would exhibit their wounds with proof.

Lady of Fatima

On May 13th 1917 there was a ten year old peasant girl, who was working in their field with her two cousins, when suddenly a lady appeared announcing she is the Lady of the Rosary. This image appeared to these specific three children every month thereafter, always on the thirteenth day, except in August when she materialized on the nineteenth. These children were interrogated and threatened by civil authorities, with their detailed stories; that their stories aroused a major curiosity within their community and surrounding communities. The August visit, Lady of the Rosary promised in October, a great miracle would happen. On October 13th, 70,000 people crowded in this field to witness the appearance of Lady of the Rosary. Consequently the Lady did appear to the children and announced herself as the Lady of the Rosary and asked for a Chapel to be built in her name.

NOTES

At the same time Lady of Rosary appeared, the crowd witnessed a beautiful solar phenomena; the sun seemed to be falling earth bound. It was a peaceful ray, a ray of hope. These visions were accepted in 1930 as appearances of the Virgin Mary by the Roman Catholic authorities but Christians were skeptical of them. The Bible never directs that Mary is to receive worship in her own right and was never respected as much as the Divine Source, even though Mary is the Jesus' Twin-flame. They also state that these episodes are too vulnerable, causing mass hysteria, and are only collective apparitions not to be convincing or reality. These are just a few subjects covered in which Christianity made up their own rules and assumptions without any evidence to prove their opinions. That is all it was to me was an opinion lacking professional evidence. This lead me into a more natural religion, the Neo-Pagan/Wicca religions were farming people who worked very hard to learn the laws of the universe. They saw how the Moon affected their lives and crops. They saw the importance of Air, Earth, Heat, and Water. These people were victims of Catholics and Protestants who prosecuted them because of appearances of their statues of the Divine Source. They said it looked too much like a demon. These people are masters of healing and herbs. I make no claim to its perfection, but I do want to make it clear that this religion does not worship the devil, nor do they perform Black Masses. These are all fictions created by organized Christianity to cast a bad light on those who worshipped in a different light. The word Witchcraft was liberally applied by the Christian church and its authorities to the native religious practices and customs that existed for thousands of years before Christianity. Many men and women died hanging and/or fire by the hands of Christians simply because of their religious expressions.

NOTES

CHAPTER II

NOTES

WICCA RELIGION

To start you off learning about the WICCA RELIGION, the Wicca calendar year starts the 20th of March, There are certain ways in which a Witch operates. One of which is their yearly calendar that is different from the standard type you use everyday. Witches have eight Sabbat (Holidays) that they celebrate, we have approximately seventy-five holidays within our yearly calendar or twelve months that we go by, however, witches do celebrate their eight holidays very similar ours.

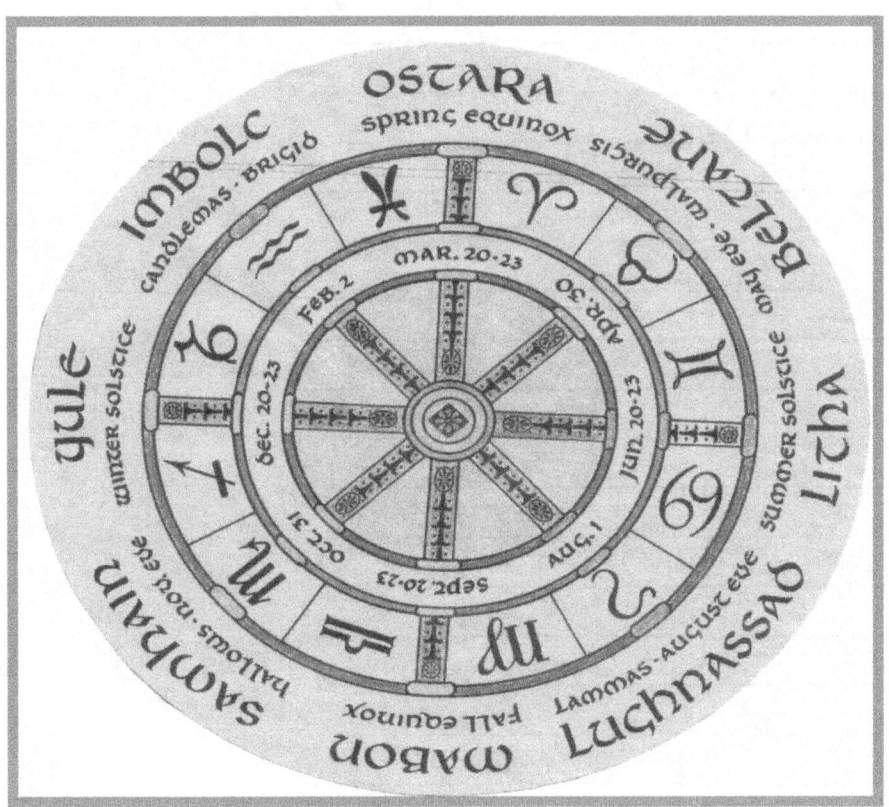

NOTES

1.   OSTARA (Spring Equinox), March 19-23, a lesser Sabbat.
The word equinox refers to the distribution of daylight and night-time hours, which are equal proportions at this festival. In classical worlds of ancient Greece and Rome, Ostera marks the beginning of the New Year for Witches. This time of the year releases the world from winter's icy grip to reveal nature's freshness, energy, rebirth, joy, and lightness. At Ostera it is a time to re-evaluate how we might have tipped the scales, and slipped from the balance point, the zero point in our lives in either one direction or another. Re-evaluation of our lives is the first stage of your Ostera spiritual work. The second stage has to do with correcting the imbalances we recognize. Over emotional results in hurt, anger, or sadness so dig deep to find what or who is causing this and rid yourself of these emotional blocks. Demons need to be cast out even your own hidden demons. Most times it is an outside source. So either eliminate your or others to become fully spiritual.

NOTES

2.   BELTANE (May Eve), May 1st, a greater Sabbat.
At Beltane, one of the primary symbolic spiritual acts is that of the Sacred Marriage, known in the world of mythology as the Heiros Gamos. Myths portray this principle through stories that feature a Hero who marries a Goddess, or when love triumphs over evil. The symbolic union between the physical polar opposites of Male and Female bodies represents the merging of universally opposite elements. Likewise, light and dark, hot and cold thus the principle of union. It is important on Beltane to be attracted to one another. There is an old adaptation of an old custom that magical folk would use to make themselves attractive at Beltane. They would pour three drops of rose oil into a large bowl, chop an apple into small pieces and add spring water ¾ the way full. Let stand for ten minutes then scoop water with hands and apply to face while saying, Awaken beauty; hold it fast, bind the mist to make it last! Day of the Maypole ceremony, Maypoles are magical phallic symbols. The ancient Celts used the Maypole as the centerpiece for dancing and fertility rites aimed at fostering fecundity in their crops and livestock. Villagers trimmed birch tree branches, then stuck them deep down into the earth, attached colorful streamers with flowers and danced. The Celts inherited this festival from the Romans, who ruled the British Isles well into the 15th century CE. At the same time of year the Roman's celebrated Flora, the Goddess of plants and flowers.

NOTES

3.   LITHA (Summer Solstice), June 19-23, a lesser Sabbat.

The Sun is at its Zenith; and paradoxically begins its decline. During Litha it is the longest day of the Solar Year. Litha occurs when the Sun enters the sign of Cancer. In Old Europe, Litha, or Midsummer was an important fire festival. In some ancient accounts, villagers would set wheels made of straw or cartwheels smeared with pitch ablaze and then roll them down hills to signify the Sun's decent, or gradual darkening, which followed this longest of days. Litha is the midpoint of the Solar Year. Symbolically speaking, this represents the midpoint of a human life. Just as the sun is at its height of power at midsummer, it also begins its decline. This is a wonderful natural metaphor for our own lives when we face the crossroads of our midlife. The sun has magical healing properties from which magical folk draw from. Traditionally practice this sun-drawing technique at sunrise or at least the first few hour of sunrise. Repeat this prayer three times. Morning Sun, take my pain; ease my heart, illness wane. Conclude this prayer by anointing your heart chakra with chamomile essential oil as you stand in the sunlight for a few moments.

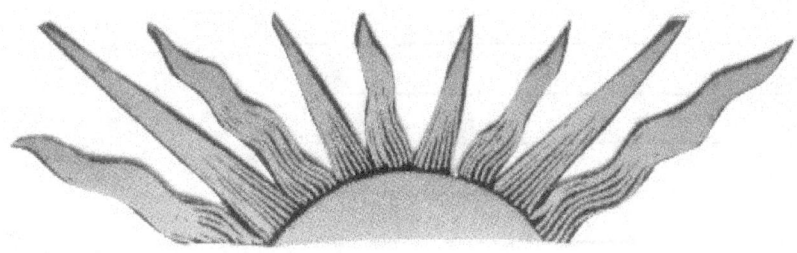

~~~~~~~~~~~NOTES~~~~~~~~~~~

4.   LAMMAS (August Eve), August 1st, a greater Sabbat.
The symbol of Lammas is sacrifice. Sacrifice involves one form of energy giving itself up so that it can transform into something else. From this perspective we can see that soil, for example, offers itself in sacrifice in order to nourish seeds. The seeds sprout then offers them self in sacrifice to become plants. Food sacrifices its energy so that it can become our bodies. It is this mystery of sacrifice, of selflessness offering that lies at the core of Lammas. Close your eyes, take several deep breaths. Imagine that you become weightless. You drift in the air and soon you feel your spirit body moving through time and space. Soon the movement stops and you find yourself in a wheat field, now your part of the field. Now bring yourself back refreshed.

NOTES

5. *MABON (Fall Equinox), September 19-23, a lesser Sabbat.*
The coming of autumn marks the end of the harvesting season. The air chills especially in the evening and morning. This time of year marks the end of your years toil. Witches follow the example of the natural world and refocuses outward directed attention toward the inner processes. In the Witches' view, autumn is not a time to initiate new projects or to start new ventures. Instead, it is a period of deep reflection when you retract goals directed efforts in order to explore the depth of your interior. Summer Equinox and Fall Equinox are balanced light. There are equal durations of night and day during the Equinoxes.

NOTES

6. *SAMHAIN (Hallows Eve), October 31, a greater sabbat.*
It is an annual festival of death that occurs at the conclusion of the Celtic Agriculture cycle. It also marks the Celtic New Year. Samhain is a Gaelic word that means "summer's End". Wisely, the ancient Celts noted that Ending and Beginning was united. Witches consider Samhain the perfect time to commence with departed loved ones since the worlds of the living and the dead are not too far apart. Samhain is a magical energy tide that unites your personal spiritual process, your individual energy system, with the universe. Each of the Sabbats offers us opportunities to shift our consciousness from personal concerns to those that are universal, collective, and archetypal. They offer us the change to move from an ordinary to a mystic mindset.

NOTES

7. *YULE (Winter Solstice), December 19-23, a lesser sabbat.*
Yule is when the sun enters the sign of Capricorn and you have officially entered winter. Witches call this second celebration in the sabbat calendar alternately the "Winter Solstice," Midwinter, and of course, Yule. The word Yule comes from the Norse Iul, which means "wheel". Yule marks the rebirth of the Sun. The "Great Wheel" of the sky. The Winter Solstice is the shortest day of the year. It is this time of the year that symbolically reminds us that light comes out of our darkness, the chaos of our lives, the heartbreak and the pain we sometimes endure. Yule is about promise. It teaches us the lessons of the mythic Phoenix that rises out of the ashes of what appears to be complete destruction. The continual rebirth of the sun illustrates that destruction is a fantasy. Life and energy go on eternally.

~~~~~~~~~~~~NOTES~~~~~~~~~~~~

8. *IMBOLC (Candlemas), February 2, a greater sabbat.*

Imbolc is the second of the Greater Sabbats in the Witches' Wheel of the Year. Imbolc is an Irish Gaelic word which is pronounced (im'-molk). Other variations are called Gaelic Imbolg and the English Candlemas-Imbolc celebrates the official end of the "Dead Time," the period from October to February, during which Witches' perform very little magic and no Initiatory Rites. This dead time coincided with the "death" of the Sun, the light of day, and subsequently all perennial plant life. Pagan folk could see that daylight hours were visibly longer at Imbolc and country folk and Witches alike celebrate this turn of events as one of awakening for the Earth's energy. One of the primary Mythic Themes of the "Great Wheel of the Year" is that of Succor; a celebration of consuming nourishment from the Goddess' body. Since the dawn of time, one of the primary images of the Goddess is that" she-who-nourishes," the ancient Goddess myths and rituals can inform us how we might come into perfect union with the female principle and her unique, spiritual form of nourishment. A woman with her baby is the basic image in mythology. Your first experience of life is that of your mother's body.

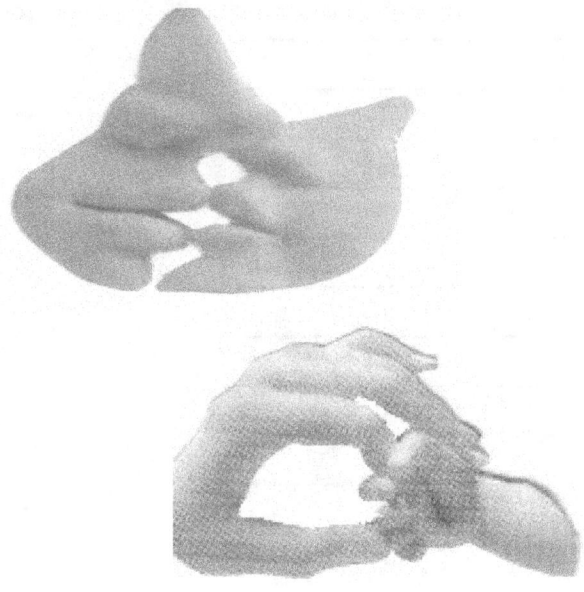

NOTES

Another very important practice of being a Witch is their Witches alphabet. Witches use this for writing out spell chants to keep their chants, spells, and workings confidential. All chants will be written this way so I recommend you memorize them fully while you do your spells. Another reason for this is to keep the left part of your brain active; your work will be that much more effective with both sides active. This is part of your training for thought are things.

WITCHES SECRET SYMBOL ALPHABET

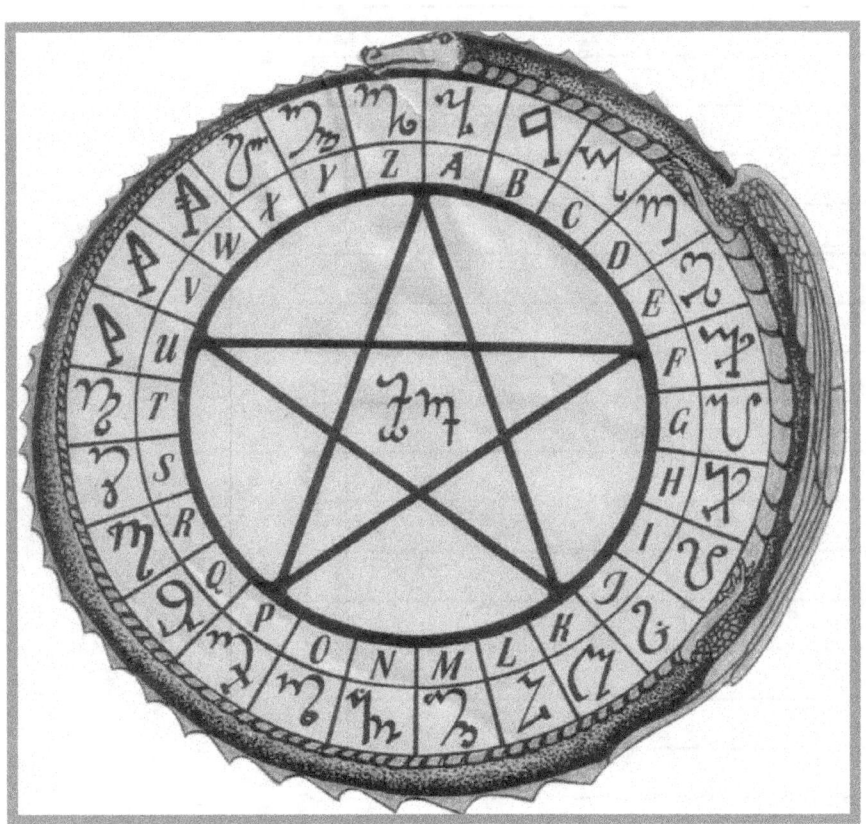

NOTES

THE WICCAN REDE

Bide the Witch's Law we must,

In perfect love, in perfect trust.

Eight words the Wiccan Rede fulfill,

"An Ye Harm None, Do What Ye Will."

What ye send forth cometh back to thee,

So ever mind the Rule of Three.

Follow this with mind and heart,

And Merry Ye Meet, and Merry Ye Part!

Aside the Ten Commandments of Christianity, this would be the only Law within the Wicca religion.

BLESSED BE
Means go toward the light and to move forward as one would say farewell, they are actually giving you a gift to move forward to which ever path you choose they'll be behind you, rooting you on!

MY ALTER

43

NOTES

- *Athame*
- *Candles- (I recommend small birthday candles so your spells doesn't take all night and never use any magic candle twice).*
    - *Sunday--------------------Lavender----------------------Healing*
    - *Monday-------------------Yellow-------------------------Meditation*
    - *Tuesday-------------------Red----------------------------Banish*
    - *Wednesday--------------Blue----------------------------Career*
    - *Thursday-----------------Green--------------------------Money*
    - *Friday---------------------Pink-----------------------------Love*
    - *Saturday------------------Brown-------------------------Wishes*
- *Chalice*
- *Frankincense*
- *Sea salt*
- *Wand*
- *Pentagrams*
- *Small dishes for all*
- *Parchment paper*

<u>WITCHES</u>

Witches use spells as a tool to become enlightened and to produce discipline in meditating, intention, and action. After a while you will not need to do spells, you will just need your thoughts. You can make anything manifest that you want. Sure its fun and entertaining, you may even obtain prestige from others, but its really not necessary. If you are attuned you will not have to use such things as spells, I do find them helpful in the beginning. I've read numerous books on witchcraft, book of Shadows, and attended numerous classes, workshops, and also teach class myself. I've reached the conclusion, that it's a lot of work and very expensive, it is a great first stepping stone. It's not the idea of doing spells, rituals, or circles daily. The idea is to get you going on your right path for enlightenment. All you need to obtain is a knowledge of yourself and know how powerful you can be. It's within your own knowledge to make things happen, just you and the Divine Source. What is very clear; Witches do not worship the devil, they do not perform infamous Black Masses, or allow themselves to become victims of sexual prey with the devil. These are all fictional, created by Christianity to cast a black light on those who worship in a different light. The Jewish religion held the secrets of the Kabala which is the source of High Magic, originally authored by the Divine Source. The Jews were forced to convert to Christianity or be killed. They pretended to convert, but continued to perform their Magic and Rituals in hiding in the countryside along with the Witches. The Witches would protect the Jews and visa versa. Witches and the Jews shared their knowledge gratefully.

NOTES

A Witch is keenly focused on the simple experiences of living in the world. They follow their heartbeats, their intuitions, their dreams, and sensations. They live their lives this way because they know that experiences of simplicity tune them into the cycles of the natural world. This is where a Witch finds power and spiritual enfoldment. In spiritual terms, darkness is only one of a variety of natural human states. To judge darkness as bad or wrong is akin to judging whether up is better than down, or whether blue is better than red. Judgment of your natural emotional state hinders your spiritual progress and your psychological wellbeing. It induces guilt and does not belong in Witches magical practices. There is no shame in having shadows; we all have them to a certain degree. It is simply a part of being human. These shadows are only your ill judgment upon yourself. Witches don't believe in death, the immortal part of you survives death.

Are you a Good Witch or Bad Witch?

NOTES

GYPSIES

Gypsies are the oldest Tarot card readers originating from India in the fourteenth century. It was actually thought they originated from Egypt. They are members of a wondering Caucasoid (from the erroneous notion that the original home of the hypothetical Indo-Europeans was the Caucasus designating or of one of the major groups of mankind: it includes peoples of Europe, North Africa, the Near East, and India. It is loosely called the White Race although it embraces many people of dark skin color with black hair). They were actually from the USSR, residing between the Black Sea and the Caspian Sea, this piece of land is called the Caucasus Belt. They then introduced the Tarot to Europe and adopted Europe as their Home. They are non-violent Transients, who dabble only divinatory, they are not considered Witches because they do not do spells or involve themselves in any rituals, ceremonies, or circles; they are considered mere Cartomanists (card readers), great musicians, and fortunetellers who loved to wander. Tarot cards actually originated from the ancient Book of Thoth, the magic book authored by the Divine Source. It was redesigned as cards during the witch hunts, to make the book portable and easily discreet to store away for reasons of safety. The book was saved from ruins of a burning temple in Egypt. It was rescued by traveling Gypsies then brought to Europe.

NOTES

EVERY MORNING GREETING
"A miracle is going to happen today".

This attracts good fortune and has a magnetic and cumulative effect. Within a short space of time, you will receive either a fantastic phone call, a letter, or you will meet someone who will change your life for the better. Whatever it is, the fact is that positive attracts. If you think positive, you will only attract positive.

"Have a Wonderful Day Everyday"

WITCH BALLS

Witch balls are symbols of growth, strength, and the cycle of life. Each color has its' own meaning. When you are ready to hang your witch ball recite this poem. Your witch ball should be cleaned every month at a full Moon and re-hung.

WITCH BALL POEM

ALL WHO GAZE UPON THIS BALL,
THEIR EVIL WISHES DO WITHDRAW.
IN MY WINDOW SHINNING BRIGHT,
PROTECT WITHIN BOTH DAY AND NIGHT!

~~~~~~~~~~~~~~NOTES~~~~~~~~~~~~~~~

ACTUALITY V. REALITY

Part of the process of becoming a reader is learning to discern "reality" from "actuality." Occultists have always maintained that everything is made up of vibrational energy. Modern scientists thoughts have finally came to the same conclusion, calling it "the wave theory." Yet, a building is still a building, and a table is still a table. Both are solid and support weight of objects. I cannot place my foot through them without damaging the building, table, or my foot. That is their reality. Still, both science and occultism insist that the building and the table (and my foot) are only vibrational energy. That is their actuality. What is actual may not appear real. Reality is, in this manual, you may read a person and their cards may mean something totally different than with another because of the vibes they are sending through the cards. In all actuality you should read their vibration more than reading the cards.

FORTUNETELLING V. DIVINITY

Fortunetelling says that something must happen. Divination never says what must happen; it only indicates what will probably happen if you continue on the path you are currently on. According to this view, you have the freedom to insure something happens or prevent it from happening. You have free will and the choice is always up to you. Fortunetelling would say that, as an example, you will have an accident in a car on a certain date. Divination would tell you that a car trip at this time could cause problems, and you are advised to stay away from cars, or proceed with caution. Fortunetelling says you have no choice you will be in the car and you will have an accident. Divination says you have free will: you can move to the train or at least stay away from cars. There is always an alternative solution with divinity. In this book, I strongly affirm free will, not predestination.

NOTES

CHAPTER III
ORIGIN OF THE TAROT

There is no proof that the tarot came from a single ancient source in Egypt, China, India or anywhere else. They were first introduced into Europe in the early 14th century is known, but where they originally came from is one of the great unprovable mysteries of the universe. India and China did have gambling systems which, to a minor extent, resembled a pack of cards. Although again, unprovable, I maintain that it is likely that a traveler going from one of those countries to the Middle Eastern, or perhaps a trader from the Middle East who went to India or China, somehow left one of these systems or versions of it, in one of the Middle Eastern countries. Then, during one of the Crusades, a knight brought back one of these proto-decks and gave it to his lord or king. Then the lord or king in a display of egotistical vanity ("I've got something you don't have!") showed it to a peer, another lord or king. That second person decided to have it duplicated. Or, in a similar manner, the artist then, showed it to another lord or king, moving from lord to lord, from king to king, the Tarot evolved. This made them interesting because these cards could inspire a relationship between humanity and the divine with mystical knowledge. The Tarot has been used as a powerful mystical and magical tool over the past several centuries. What you need to do is to start yourself learning one suit at a time, for about a week with each suit. As you go through the weeks acclimate each suit until you have learned your complete deck. Then you need to apply psycometry, meditation, and consistency. Eventually you can even have mediumship come through as it does for me. Each spread is numbered within the illustrations.

NOTES

MAJOR ARCANE

FOOL ....*TRUST*................................... *fresh start, short trip, risks*
MAGICIAN ....*ENERGY*............................*resource, skills and knowledge*
H.PRIESTESS.........*INTUITION*..........................*useful advice, psychic abilities*
EMPRESS.............*CREATIVITY*..............*problem solve, power with loving hand*
EMPEROR ....*ACHIEVEMENT*.......*legal situation, see whole picture then act*
HIEROPHANT ......*TRADITION*...............*male spirit guide, establish own design*
LOVERS................*ATTRACTION*..........*do well, indecisive about two allurements*
CHARIOT ....*DETERMINED*.........*self confident, clever escape, take control*
STRENGTH ....*BRAVE* ....*show kindness, faced with fear act calmly*
HERMIT...............*INTROSPECTION*......*experienced, answers are coming to you*
WHEEL................*CYCLES*............................*karma, what is sent comes back*
JUSTICE..............*TRUTH*........................... *impartial, justice will triumph*
HANGMAN...........*SUSPENSION*..............*need to wait, perspectives are required*
DEATH................*TRANSFORMATION*...*major change, if resisted may be painful*
TEMPERANCE......*PATIENCE*..............*precise timing, patients the future awaits*
DEVIL.................*TRICKERY*............ *protect yourself, deceitful person, warning*
TOWER...............*CRISIS*..................*you're on top, change is here, you'll go on*
STAR..................*ILLUMINATION*......*avoid negativity, it's you're story, right path*
MOON.................*JOURNEY*..............*separate illusion from reality, remodeling*
SUN...................*RADIANCE*..................*show the world who you are and done*
JUDGMENT ....*RECKONING*.............*right decisions, start a whole new plan*
WORLD..............*CONCLUSION*....................*the world can be yours, go for it*

NOTES

The Celtic Cross symbolizes the Christian Cross, erected throughout Ireland.

1. You
2. Present conditions
3. Obstacles
4. Their basis
5. Past conditions
6. Your goals
7. How others see you
8. Final outcome

NOTES

CUPS

ACE ……………..LOVE………………………..unconditional love, positive emotions

TWO……………..ROMANCE……………………....a lucky day, unity in this romance

THREE……………CELEBRATION……….you're of truth, joy, creativity, celebration

FOUR……………..RE-EVALUATE……………dissatisfied, gain insight, value system

FIVE………………DISSAPOINTMENT…walk away, lost love , gained in experience

SIX…………………JOY…………………………………….loyal friends, a gift, short trip

SEVEN ……………ILLUSION……………………....clear choices, no wishful thinking

EIGHT ……………SACRIFICE……………….....is it worth it, too much time on others

NINE …………….FULFILLMENT……....content, make wish, very lucky time for you

TEN………………SUCCESS……………peers respect and honor you for good actions

PRINCESS ………TENDERNESS……………show concerns, new love, pay attention

PRINCE ………….CHARM……………….what's in it for them? Watch for deceit

QUEEN…………...EMPATHY……………...help someone without expecting returns

KING……………..CONSIDERATION……….be sincerely understanding, make efforts

NOTES

RELATIONSHIP

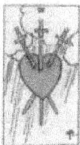

1. How you see your love
2. How your love sees you
3. Your needs
4. Their needs
5. Relationship now
6. Where you would like it to go
7. Where they want it to go
8. Final outcome

NOTES

WANDS

ACE ....INITIATION....................*reply from an aggressive resume,*

TWO ....PLANNING.................... *calm, family issues, sibling rivalry*

THREE...............OPPORTUNITY................*business, south, happy enterprise*

FOUR ....COMPLETION..................*close a deal, satisfaction and honor*

FIVE...................COMPETITION..........*opponent, devoted, stand up for yourself*

SIX......................VICTORY................*recognize / celebrate, victory approaching*

SEVEN...............COURAGE................*spite fear, start new biz, maybe forbidden*

EIGHT ....SIGNALS..............................*pay attention, do it do it now!*

NINE..................DISCIPLINE..........................*tactful, prepare your position*

TEN....................OPPRESSION.............*show energy, schooling, over committed*

PRINCESS...........IMPULSIVENESS.........*watch spending, wild at times, trip west*

PRINCE ....AMBITION........................*risks, change of residence, wedding*

QUEEN...............INSPIRATION................*true friends with radiant and charisma*

KING..................DYNAMIC.......................*partnership, self employ, north bound*

NOTES

TURNING POINT

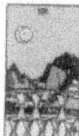   

1. *Surrounding circumstances*
2. *What you need to know*
3. *Your belief pattern*
4. *Bridge leading to this point*
5. *Turning point*
6. *Unexpected benefits*
7. *What you learned*
8. *What will evolve*
9. *Windfall*
10. *Possible outcome*
11. *Second outcome*

NOTES

PENTACLES

ACE……………….REWARDS……………………….new business, signing contracts

TWO……………....CHANGE………………... …..don't worry, be flexible, changes

THREE……………..WORK…………………...female spirit guide, teamwork is needed

FOUR………………POSSESSIVE……………..security comes from within, not selfish

FIVE……………….ANXIETY………………...express you're feelings, a time of testing

SIX…………………GENEROSITY……………....give to receive, the ten fold method

SEVEN…………….FRUSTRATION……….think positive the outcome will be positive

EIGHT…………….CRAFTMANSHIP….skilled, promotions, tentative to small details

NINE………………ABUNDANCE………resources, ideas, independence and freedom

TEN……………...PROTECTION……………..protect what is dear, a trip eastbound

PRINCESS………..PRACTICAL…………………….watch glamour, too enticing

PRINCE…………..RELIABILITY…………speak clearly with stubbornness and trust

QUEEN…………...GOOD FORTUNE…………...protect and hide money, time to save

KING……………...PRAGMATISM……………………..watch coercion, self discipline

NOTES

CAREER

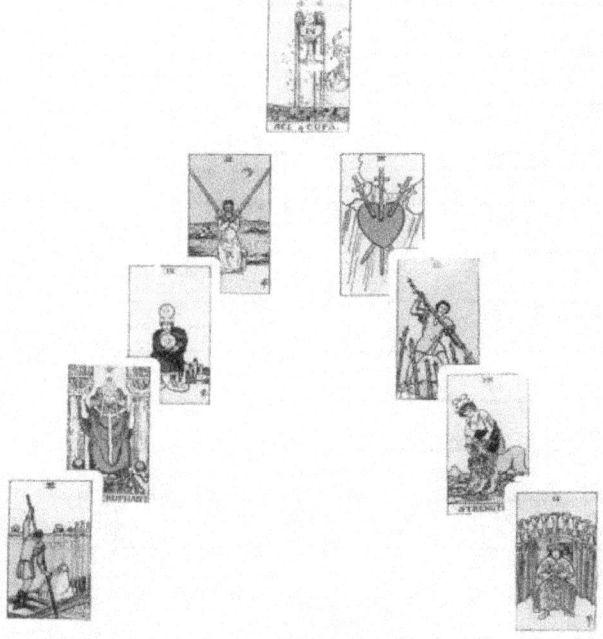

1 – 3 Current situation
4 – 6 Past influences
7 – 9 Future outcome

NOTES

SWORDS

ACE................. TRIUMPH……………………………..cut thru lies, karma

TWO.................BALANCE……………..new partnership, no need to struggle

THREE…………....SORROW……avoid self-pity, someone has destroyed your trust

FOUR………………SECLUSION………………no-one helps, strategic withdrawal

FIVE……………..DEFEAT…………………………..without regrets, surrender

SIX……………….PASSAGE……better times, liberating solutions to old problems

SEVEN…………..OPPOSITION………strength and wise, do not resort to trickery

EIGHT……………INDECISION………………no decision, concentrate on clarity

NINE…………....NIGHTMARE…………………a bad situation, personal demons

TEN……………..RUIN………………….. sickness, healing required, seek a doctor

PRINCESS…........IDEAS…………………………. you see weak spots in planning

PRINCE………….INGENUITY…………...teacher, schooling will appear in your life

QUEEN…………..INDEPENDENCE……..too much info, write it down for accurate

KING…………….INTELLECT……….don't brown nose, share your thoughts, smart

NOTES

MOVING ON

1 – 2 *Moving away from*
3 – 4 *Moving toward*
5 – 6 *What to consider before taking action*
7 – 8 *Reasons to move on*
9   *Final outcome*

NOTES

ANNUAL SPREAD

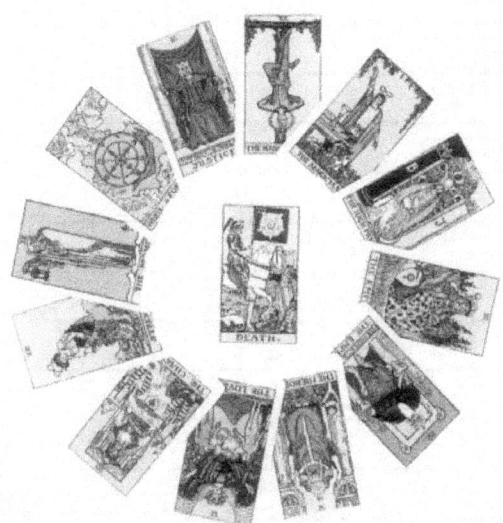

1. January outcome
2. February outcome
3. March outcome
4. April outcome
5. May outcome
6. June outcome
7. July outcome
8. August outcome
9. September outcome
10. October outcome
11. November outcome
12. December outcome
13. Yearly outcome

NOTES

WEEKLY SPREAD

1. Sunday outcome
2. Monday outcome
3. Tuesday outcome
4. Wednesday outcome
5. Thursday outcome
6. Friday outcome
7. Saturday outcome

NOTES

ASTROLOGY AND TAROT

Astrology is very important in a tarot reading, it identifies important people in your lives, your compatibilities, their traits, and yours. I listed these signs pertaining to the major arcane.

- ARIES……………………………EMPEROR
- TAURUS…………………………HEIROPHANT
- GEMINI…………………………..LOVERS
- CANCER…………………………CHARIOT
- LEO……………………………....STRENGTH
- VIRGO…………………………...HERMIT
- LIBRA……………………………JUSTICE
- SCORPIO……………………......DEATH
- SAGITTARIUS………………….TEMPERANCE
- CAPRICORN……………………DEVIL
- AQUARIUS……………………...STAR
- PISCES…………………………..MOON

Cups……………………*Relationships*
Wands…………………..*Learning*
Pentacles………………*Career*
Swords…………………*Conflicts*

NOTES

CHAPTER IV

KARMA DEBT

Karma Debt, the influences of your past lives, they are barriers that we bury deep within that needs to be corrected. We must correct these in order to pursue our evolution and to seek a more superior spiritual consciousness. If we fail to involve ourselves in spiritual work during this life time, we will have to return to the same senero and face the same obstacles. This part of my book will show you our weaknesses and the ground work in which we build our future. The following will show and help you acknowledge the baggage you have brought along from past lives and master its effects. To start you off, first you need to study yourself by your astrological sun or birth sign found below with the dates, they may be a little negative, but I wrote it this way for you to correct what needs to be corrected within your self, just remember my sign is in here as well, and this too is not pretty. Second, by finding your date given below, you'll find your opposite sign or your rising sign, this is where your Karma debt lies, why you act the way you do, and what you need to correct in this life, within your personality to move to a higher spiritual level so you won't have to repeat the same mistakes in your next life. Third, within your Karma debt reveals your past life in order for you to understand what traits you carry over from that life into this life. I've tried to make it as simple as possible for you to understand so you don't have to analyze it or pick it apart to receive the information you need to further your growth.

NOTES

DATE AND DEBT

01-01-1900 to 01-20-1901----------------------Sagittarius
01-21-1901 to 07-21-1902----------------------Scorpio
07-22-1902 to 01-15-1904----------------------Libra
01-16-1904 to 09-18-1905----------------------Virgo
09-19-1905 to 03-30-1807----------------------Leo
03-31-1807 to 09-27-1908----------------------Cancer
09-28-1908 to 03-23-1910----------------------Gemini
03-24-1910 to 12-08-1912----------------------Taurus
12-24-1912 to 06-06-1913----------------------Aries
06-07-1913 to 12-03-1914----------------------Pisces
12-04-1915 to 05-31-1916----------------------Aquarius
06-01-1916 to 02-13-1918----------------------Capricorn
02-14-1918 to 08-15-1919----------------------Sagittarius
08-16-1919 to 02-07-1921----------------------Scorpio
02-08-1921 to 08-22-1922----------------------Libra
08-23-1922 to 08-27-1922----------------------Virgo
08-28-1922 to 08-31-1922----------------------Libra
09-01-1922 to 04-22-1924----------------------Leo
10-27-1925 to 04-16-1927----------------------Cancer
04-17-1927 to 12-28-1928----------------------Gemini
12-29-1928 to 07-07-1930----------------------Taurus
07-08-1930 to 12-28-1931----------------------Aries
12-29-1931 to 06-24-1933----------------------Pisces
06-25-1933 to 03-08-1935----------------------Aquarius
03-09-1935 to 09-14-1936----------------------Capricorn
09-15-1936 to 03-03-1938----------------------Sagittarius
03-04-1938 to 09-11 1939----------------------Scorpio
09-12-1939 to 05-24-1941----------------------Libra
05-25-1941 to 11-21-1942----------------------Virgo
11-22-1942 to 05-11-1944----------------------Leo
05-12-1944 to 12-02-1945----------------------Cancer
12-03-1945 to 08-02-1947----------------------Gemini
08-03-1947 to 01-25-1949----------------------Taurus
01-26-1949 to 07-26-1950----------------------Aries
07-27-1950 to 03-28-1952----------------------Pisces
03-29-1952 to 10-09-1953----------------------Aquarius
10-10-1953 to 04-02-1955----------------------Capricorn

NOTES

04-03-1955 to 10-04-1956	Sagittarius
10-05-1956 to 06-16-1958	Scorpio
06-17-1958 to 12-15-1959	Libra
12-16-1959 to 06-10-1961	Virgo
06-11-1961 to 12-23-1962	Leo
12-24-1962 to 08-25-1964	Cancer
08-26-1964 to 02-19-1966	Gemini
02-20-1966 to 08-19-1967	Taurus
08-20-1967 to 04-19-1969	Aries
04-20-1969 to 11-02-1970	Pisces
11-03-1970 to 04-27-1972	Aquarius
04-28-1972 to 10-27-1973	Capricorn
10-28-1973 to 07-10-1975	Sagittarius
07-11-1975 to 01-07-1977	Scorpio
01-08-1977 to 07-05-1978	Libra
07-06-1978 to 01-05-1980	Virgo
01-06-1980 to 01-07-1980	Leo
01-08-1980 to 01-12-1980	Virgo
01-13-1980 to 09-20-1981	Leo
09-21-1981...............	Cancer
09-22-1981 to 09-24-1981	Leo
09-25-1981 to 03-16-1983	Cancer
03-17-1983 to 09-11-1984	Gemini
09-12-1984 to 04-06-1986	Taurus
04-07-1986 to 05-05-1986	Aries
05-06-1986 to 05-08-1986	Taurus
05-09-1986 to 12-02-1987	Aries
12-03-1987 to 05-22-1989	Pisces
05-23-1989 to 11-18-1990	Aquarius
11-19-1990 to 08-01-1992	Capricorn
08-02-1992 to 02-01-1994	Sagittarius
02-02-1994 to 07-31-1995	Scorpio
08-01-1995 to 01-25-1997	Libra
01-26-1997 to 10-20-1998	Virgo
10-21-1998 to 04-09-2000	Leo
04-10-2000 to 10-13-2001	Cancer
10-14-2001 to 04-13-2003	Gemini
04-14-2003 to 12-26-2004	Taurus
12-27-2004 to 06-22-2006	Aries
06-23-2006 to 12-18-2007	Pisces

NOTES

12-19-2007 to 08-21-2009----------------------Aquarius
08-22-2009 to 03-03-2011----------------------Capricorn
03-04-2011 to 08-30-2012----------------------Sagittarius
08-31-2012 to02-18-2014----------------------Scorpio
02-19-2014 to 11-12-2015----------------------Libra
11-13-2015 to 05-09-2017----------------------Virgo
05-10-2017 to 11-06-2018----------------------Leo
11-07-2018 to 05-05-2020----------------------Cancer
05-06-2020 to 01-18-2022----------------------Gemini
01-19-2022 to 07-17-2023----------------------Taurus
07-18-2023 to 01-11-2025----------------------Aries
01-12-2025 to 07-27-2026----------------------Pisces
07-28-2026 to 03-26-2028----------------------Aquarius
03-27-2028 to 09-23-2029----------------------Capricorn
09-24-2029 to 03-21-2031----------------------Sagittarius
03-22-2031 to 12-02-2032----------------------Scorpio
12-03-2032 to 06-03-2034----------------------Libra
06-04-2034 to 11-30-2035----------------------Virgo
12-01-2035 to 05-29-2037----------------------Leo
05-30-2037 to 02-10-2039----------------------Cancer
02-11-2039 to 08-11-2040----------------------Gemini
08-12-2040 to 02-04-2042----------------------Taurus
02-05-2042 to 08-18-2043----------------------Aries
08-19-2043 to 04-18-2045----------------------Pisces
04-19-2045 to 10-18-2046----------------------Aquarius
10-19-2046 to 04-12-2048----------------------Capricorn
04-13-2048 to 12-14-2049----------------------Sagittarius
12-15-2049 to 12-21-2049----------------------Scorpio
12-22-2049 to 12-23-2049----------------------Sagittarius
12-24-2049 to 12-31-2050----------------------Scorpio

NOTES

LIBRA WITH A PAST LIFE OF ARIES

(None of the Above)

You are considered the month of <u>Visual Expression</u>; you carry with you the scales which symbolizes justice, equilibrium, and balance. You can be so bright that it blurs distinctions between bad and good. You visualize through the light that all are equal, and this causes uncertainty and indecisiveness. Making decisions or judgments, present major trouble for you. You strive for equilibrium and harmony in your relationships and environment, but usually find yourself confused. You mull over things obsessively considering every angle of an issue in an attempt to reach an equal state. You perpetually hesitate, wavering between one aspect and the other. You do see both sides to a story, but you seem to hold equal merit. You become paralyzed with the fear of making decisions by default. You rarely take a decisive action, when you do, you find yourself moving in circles, retracing your steps, or revisiting old decisions, filled with anxiety that you neglected to consider every possibility, you can never leave well enough alone. You go through strenuous activity and make great progress but, as soon as the pressure diminishes, you become uncertain again and proceed to undo what you have already accomplished. You are very friendly, open, warm, sympathetic, and social. You are a great listener and encourage other to confide in you. You enjoy caring for others, and as soon as someone shows the slightest need, you will be there to lend a hand. You must let others know you do not make good decisions for their problems, you freeze up. As an Aries in your previous life, you are self confident, but your high opinion of your self leads to many disappointments. Preoccupied with yourself, you waste energy and are in an almost constant state of agitation. Although you work, you never build anything solid. You overreact to failure, assume an aggressive attitude, and often grapple with problems in very narrow-minded ways. This brings about a profound sense of frustration, which presently provokes an aggressiveness that often puzzles those close to you. You will need to point yourself toward sacrificing in its noblest sense to free yourself from frustration, and to move along your path with devotion to a cause beyond yourself and your ego that you have placed within your limited circle of friends, which restricts your opportunities for sharing, or being part of a team so you will regain your equilibrium. You will also need to consider what others say and open yourself to the possibility that their opinions have merit. This will soften your personality and you will become more capable of mastering your anger. As you come to understand that the group's success is more important than your own, you will experience real happiness. Through this sort of unselfishness, you can accomplish your improvement and find peace.

NOTES

SCORPIO WITH A PAST LIFE IN TAURUS

(A Bitter Trail)

Your month represents the _God of War_. Your judgment can be cruel and harsh, and unfeeling. You can burn like fire, but combined with mercy however, judgment has great healing potential. You emanate a powerful magnetism while at the same time you appear cold and reserved. You can be charming, bewitching, even hypnotizing. People are very uneasy around you because they feel your magnetism and don't quite know what it is. You are very courageous, but you get your blood too fired up. As soon as you sense danger you go into high gear, ready for any encounter, and when you strike, you go straight for the heart. You are strong, spiritually and physically and are endowed with the willpower to attain whatever goals you set for yourself. You are extremely independent, but do not feel comfortable unless you are in control and have the upper hand. Your determination is rivaled only by your impatience. Your weakness is your sexual organs, that portion of the anatomy that is so a powerful influence human behavior, in both genders, you are deemed sexy, but both can easily become destructive in the use of your sexual power. You love melodramatic stories and are gratified by extreme emotions. While you yearn for love, you do not display your need for love. Your jealousy is legendary; you simply cannot stand to see someone else with something you want. Your envy is all the more dangerous because it only subtly expresses itself. You can be so consumed by envy that you shower your unsuspecting victim with negativity. Having you as an enemy can be devastating. You are not very logical, and you immediately discern other people's weaknesses, and will not hesitate to openly reveal them, if I wanted to know the worst aspect about myself I would just ask a Scorpio. You can be profoundly generous and giving only to make your victim more dependent and subordinate. Your giving is not sharing in the true sense it is only performed to gain control. You change from blind love to fierce hate in no time at all. You easily blame your distress on others, and take out your anxieties on the people around you. You have to remember the boomerang effect; that one day you will receive exactly what you give. You must give up the intention of settling the scores, just let it go. What goes around comes around. You must think things through before you act. You must become more sensitive to other's needs, and to detach yourself from your emotions whenever you experience a surge of anger, passion, or hatred, you must endeavor to control it. You must also stop manufacturing crisis's and dramas that eventually overwhelm you. You are firmly attached to a certain way of seeing the world; you are stubborn, slow, and extremely reluctant to change. Susceptible to body pleasures, you are completely a pleasure-seeking individual. You are in love with beauty and nature, are extremely possessive, and pursue material rather than spiritual assets.

NOTES

Fearful of the loss of your own comfort, you cut yourself off from meaningful experiences. Your life is routine and empty. You're folded in by stubbornness; you neither listen nor learn from others. At this time you must do what it takes to achieve genuine transformation by abandoning the rigid rules that mark your life and allow spontaneity to enter, tasting freedom of action. This way you will become aware of the illusions that burden your spirit, trusting the light to protect you. This could prove to be a difficult improvement, it may cause some material losses, initially, your comfort and sense of security may feel threatened but if you want to accomplish your improvement you will have to pay the price. As time goes on you will become more independent in your actions. You not only have to improve these qualities of Scorpio but the Taurus sign as well. You are the hardest sign for improvement and I suggest you make a list from all of your improvement as you correct them to make sure you've conquered the all corrections within this life time.

NOTES

SAGITTARIUS WITH A PAST LIFE IN GEMINI

(Like a Rainbow)

Your sign means encouragement, sustenance, or assistance, and sharing. I suggest within this life time you find security, well-being, and hope, if you're to allow yourself to slip into any complacency and self-righteousness. All in all, you are extremely a positive individual. Your sign means the rainbow which symbolizes hope and new beginnings. You are propelled by fire like a rocket, by a force deep within your spirit. Due to this inner fire, you constantly seek challenges and risks. This daredevil quality that you possess has both bad and good effects. This adventurous behavior, if not balanced by good judgment can make you very irresponsible. Testing yourself is the only thing that interests you. You will even go out of you way to make a particular test more difficult. Like cramming for a test the night before and passing it with flying colors. Rather than causing anxiety, this added pressure brings out the best in you. You need to feel pressure in order to succeed. The pressure nourishes you, without it, you lose interest very quickly. You seize every opportunity to perform heroically and are constantly striving to extend your own limits. You do not focus on the goals themselves, but on the means of deriving maximum pleasure from the undertaking. Though you intend no harm, you are preoccupied with proving yourself and can be insensitive to the doubts and fears of those around them. You are generally intelligent, or at least rational. You focus on the essentials. You love to learn new things but you dislike rigidity of any kind and tend to seek their education in unconventional settings. You love freedom and cannot stay in one place for a long time. You prefer to explore new horizons, both physical and intellectual, this wonder lust applies to relationships as well, periodically needing to rediscover your partner. If you feel your relationship is too routine, you feel its too difficult for you to stay. You are critical of your own behavior and always look for fault within yourself, immediately taking full responsibility for your actions, never placing blame on others. You do not hold grudges, are not resentful, and are quick to forgive because you are more focused on your own inadequacies and failures. You not only learn from your mistakes but those mistakes of others and use this as a learning process, which for you this is a constant improvement throughout this life time. With a past life as a Gemini, you have the duality characteristic, considering your life from two opposing viewpoints, you live with deep uncertainty. Decision making is your major obstacle. You cannot establish a definite course of action and stick to it. Another one of your problems is your lack of concentration, which makes you appear superficial. Your instability hinders your efforts in attaining a professional standard which handicaps your spiritual and physical evolution.

NOTES

To be accepted in a group you dance to any tune and because of your "chameleon" tendency, you are often called a hypocrite. You are faced with challenges; you have to redefine your aim and accomplish them. Your responsibilities and obligations are opportunities to solidify your own opinions. You must not turn your back on reality; you must confront it with loyalty. In fact, you will be so eager for justice that integrity, sincerity, and your refusal to compromise will become central issues in your evolution. You can find your own identity, authenticity which will be at the heart of your commitment and discover your true mission on Earth, sharing your wisdom and revealing truth.

NOTES

CAPRICORN WITH A PAST LIFE IN CANCER

(Living in the Material World)

You are the sign furthest from the sun and because of this distance you are considered the sign that <u>Nurtures Delusions</u>. You are however, a very spiritual sign because you are linked to the 72 channels of energy through which Light descends into the world. You also connect to the element of water, which is the symbol of mercy. You sometimes prematurely abandon your dreams to face the cold realities of adulthood, because of this, in later years you may feel you were deprived of something. You are generally a serious person and do not give of yourself readily. You feel people are responsible for their own lives and everything has to be earned which gives you an uncharitable view of the world. This inner spiritual energy I stated you have has a dry and cold quality which causes hardness for you to express your feelings or to give or receive love. This lack of warmth is present throughout you life causing you to keep your feeling buried deep within your soul. You are the most materialistic sign of the universe, all you thoughts and feelings are connected to the physical matter. You are extremely independent and do not tolerate authority. You are very demanding, both of yourself and others. You are reliable, but move slowly, step by step, in order to protect yourself. You can see both spiritual and material purposes of life, but seldom take full advantage of your unique perspective and just dwell on the material side of things, but the potential for seeing the spiritual dimension is always present. We are all made of, physical matter and spirit, body and soul, a beautiful combination of the physical and the metaphysical. You must not remain attached to only one of these two combinations to exclude the other because you begin to discern a positive direction. Where there is potential for negativity, there is also the greatest potential for manifestation of the Light. Though the light is blocked, or distant, or filtered, the potential for receiving its blessing is still there. You have enormous spiritual, if you want to develop it. You must understand that nothing acquired in the physical world is the result of your own merit, hard work, or determination. The source of all these things is the Light. If you continue to confine your desires to material things, you will remain unsatisfied and frustrated. You also must share, the more you share, the more energy you reveal, and the more accomplished you feel. You must reveal your true nature, which is sensitive and humane. By turning your determination and perseverance to service others, you will develop new and satisfying spiritual abilities. You will start to understand that work is an opportunity to reveal good, and not drudgery attached to an eventual material reward. These traits are carried on from your past life as a Cancer, so not only do you have to improve these traits but those presented with a Cancer. Cancer inherits the burden of doubt and because of this trait you deal with the constant anxiety.

NOTES

You seek security to the extent that you idealize life and because of this you manage either to conceal your problems, or to eagerly accept the direction of others, thus rejecting every kind of responsibility. As a consequence, you are the ultimate conformist. You never really open up to the possibilities of the outside world. You live like a hermit, buried in your own world, relying on materialism for security. Because of this, you unfairly make them a scapegoat for all your weaknesses. You can transfer this regard and effort for society as a whole. You must not refuse to grow, or assuming infantile behavior, or ever taking risks. In order to achieve security, you must organize your life according to rules and laws of society, which could make you a patriot or at least a politician. Your improvement will teach you maturity to cut the umbilical cord with family, and to accept your responsibilities to look for new ways to dispel your anxieties. By doing this you will taste the pleasures of risk taking and commit yourself without forethought and find a worthy cause and identify with it. You will be to fulfill your Spiritual mission in life.

NOTES

AQUARIUS WITH A PAST LIFE IN LEO

(Under Water)
You are both the channel for appeasing the world and the sign of abundance; everything is poured out and shared, no exceptions. You manifest equilibrium and balance with force of benediction or approval, giving you the opportunity to reveal truth and Light. You are considered the <u>Month of Redemption</u>. You spend your life tearing down structures and systems that you've built. You are unique, which makes it difficult for any one to ignore you. You main objective is to strive to change the universe through your original ideas. You support grand global causes, but often fail to help those who are suffering nearby. You rather deal with social rights of an entire nation rather than with problems of close friends because you lack the sense of the practical and are too passionately independent and private. Despite your friendliness and open-mindedness, you are considered the most stubborn of all signs. You reject all established structures, whether in marriage or in business. You fight to maintain your individuality and freedom in order to exercise your innovative ideas. You detest contentment and destroy all limitations in your path. Your thickest walls you encounter are often those of your own ego. Even though you start to make changes in your life physically, you remain unchanged deep within you heart. You do, however, have the strength to break through the constraints of the physical world because of your high level of consciousness. You can certainly help humanity as long as your ideas do not become more important than the cause itself. You must learn that caring about society does not mean neglecting any individual. True spirituality means being a part of humanity, not above it. You are merely a channel for this energy and, therefore, are not entitled to personal glory. As a Leo in you previous life you will cause certain obstacles in relationships. In marriage, for example, you must slowly but surely abandon your preoccupation with your own selfish desires. You will have to exchange your sacrosanct independence for a new concept of life: interdependence. This world is not "you" versus all others but that we are all equal on the same level. If you give up honors and glamour, you will succeed in creating an immense restriction and take control of the duality of your correction in you personal life and your humanitarian mission. You are a true missionary. You can attain the consciousness of a cosmic reality and feel responsible for humanity as a whole. You can know true friendship and perhaps even universal fraternity. Because you've inherited the lion role you have the power and the strength to accomplish this task. Your correction will be never to over dominate your subjects. You live in the limelight where you flash your luxury which for you, will not be easy to be without, but you must! Moreover, overcoming your pride also will not an easy thing to accomplish either, again you must.

NOTES

When you face difficulties in your marriage and reinforcing, accepting partnership as an equal with whom you share everything, this will be your preliminary drill to overcome your pride. By accomplishing this task you will seek the admiration you so deserve. You also have to deplete your arrogance to exploit your power to control others. Because you consider yourself the center of the universe, you will need to reverse this for love and gratitude without struggling with reality and find your spiritual path. Oh yes, you must delete that enormous ego by practicing humility and modesty while living in simplicity.

NOTES

PISCES WITH A PAST LIFE IN VIRGO

(Born to Share)
You are considered the back bone to all the signs, without you the Zodiac would fall apart. You are linked to the world below, the world of illusions. You are also considered the <u>Month of Joy</u>. You are balanced with justice, equilibrium, purity, and mercy. It is said that great spirits, who have very little improvements left to do, reincarnate into Pisceans. You are the humblest sign of the Zodiac and naturally yield to others. You are very sensitive and feel vibrations and emotions of events unfolding around you. You take on others suffering and problems as if they were your own. For this reason, people love to confide in you, knowing they will find comfort and support. You must remember not to allow your sensitivity to get the upper hand. You must remember it is essential to tell others what is wrong, so they may confront their problems as their first step toward their own improvements. Because you are so humble you lack the substance to fight for what you desire and difficult to obtain it. You are well aware that everything in the world is an illusion, that everything has already been decided, and that the suffering of the world is only temporary. This passive, reactive perception of the world often leads to a complacent life, like a fish in an aquarium. You have to remind yourself that the reason that you are here is to manifest the Light, and without action no Light can be revealed. As I said prior, you are connected to two worlds, the upper and the lower, an exact balance between the physical worlds, because you are human, and the spiritual world, because you have evolved from a different sphere of consciousness. You could pass from one world to another very easily, grasping the spirit. To obtain this level, however, you must take action and also improve the qualities from your past life as a Virgo and as a Virgo, you have a hard time detaching yourself from logic; you think and live in a reasonable world. You have difficulties "seeing the forest through the trees." You are absorbed in intricate rationalizations, which, although right in the beginning, do not satisfy you after all because you only saw one side of the picture (the physical one). You're concerned for details turned you into an irascible and fussy person. Having fallen into excessive organizing, you lost all trace of spontaneity. This behavior causes you difficulties and disagreements in your sexual life. Due to your unwillingness to get emotionally involved for fighting the fact causes you to be afraid of not having control with a relationship, causing emotional outbursts of any kind. You have a very rigid way of thinking, and unable to listen and learn from others because you demand factual perfection. You can make your tasks more difficult than it should be. You also aim too high causing you to lose your self-confidence. To understand and master your own life you must not classify and label according to your strict rules.

NOTES

In this life your problem is to try to put the pieces back together that you've left fragmented in your past life...First you must understand that a spiritual reality is the origin of everything physical.. Give up analyzing the effects and you will perceive the cause. Dropping your requirement for logical explanations will enable you to erase the doubt that has troubled you for so long. Along this path, you will gain an image of the world that goes beyond the senses and open doors to a more spiritual level of consciousness. You will experience emotions that will help you change your perception of others; by judging them less, they will offer you more. This will ignite in you a love for your fellow beings and reinforce your compassion. Finally you will learn to act on two levels. You can live in the present while looking into the future.

NOTES

ARIES WITH A PAST LIFE IN LIBRA

(Rebel without a cause)

You are known as the <u>God of War</u> within your ruling month and are also known for its confrontations, battles, and potential antagonism. You must through this life time try to strive to diminish your desire to receive for your self alone. Your strengths and weaknesses are seeds of infancy, or immaturity, coupled with the tendency of impulsiveness, and stubbornness, and a love of freedom with total disregard for the consequences of your actions. You tend to think of yourself as the center of the universe, and when you want something, you want it now. You are considered very daring within confrontations and would even stoop to seek them out for fear of your enormous ego being threatened. If you're not the center of the universe than no-one can be either. You will try to destroy them out by using your ungraceful ego against others humbleness and attack them. This is not a very attractive trait of yours and this is the most important improvement you must make to be totally spiritually evolved throughout this life time. Your ego must be destroyed by yourself and no-one else. You merely need to walk away from it and leave it behind; you need to master your ego. You are often in a role as an arbitrator, but you are unable to settle conflicts because you refuse to make difficult decisions. Taking sides is difficult for you since it implies you possibly hurting someone. So rather than making a clear choice, you try to unite what is incompatible only for you to suffer the consequences of your own indecisions. As a Libra you learned to compromise in order to avoid any confrontations. You are overly dependent on the opinion of others, and this often caused you to behave aggressively soon after your initial act of submission; classic passive aggressive behavior. Your improvement must first and foremost, uncover your identity, your unique needs, and your individual desires. You must seek independence and reinforce your self confidence. This will help you discover your own spiritual nature and enable you to become more proactive in all areas in your life. Along this path of improvement, you must stop avoiding confrontations and face them as they unfold, without the approval of others. As you pass each test you should gain awareness and confidence, knowing your own true personality and strength. By combining Libra's unselfishness with Aries's ability to "fight the good fight" you will bring an overall evolution of your soul, allowing you to become the cause of fulfillment you soon receive. Your weak point is your head, you rush into everything head first, without thinking of the consequences.

NOTES

TAURUS WITH A PAST LIE IN SCORPIO

(Bull in the Bubble)

Your nickname for this month is the <u>Month of Light</u>, ruled by Venus (the only planet to rotate in a clockwise direction, which results in a hidden spiritual energy, because Venus moves from left to right from the spiritual energy of judgment it also moves toward the spiritual energy of mercy), this is why its called the planet of love and beauty, because you correct a dark situation beautifully and with the utmost love. You are the force of judgment present in the universe. So you must combine both light and judgment and the take the best advantage of all possibilities. The first thing you must do is step toward understanding your strengths and weaknesses. Your first weakness is you don't like looking for trouble nor make waves, just live and let live. You think that things will work itself out in the end. You are too satisfied with the cards you are dealt which makes you very loyal, consistent, patient, tolerant, law-abiding, friendly, dependable, and non-judgmental. You prefer to be left alone in your comfortable bliss without any drastic change because the Light is very warm on your back. The world you live in as a Taureans are bathed in Light, Light is everywhere, beautiful, dazzling, but sometimes blinding, because of this you tend to be an eternal optimist, whatever happens, you focus only on the positive and disregard the negative. Nothing seems to upset you; you even refuse to attribute bad intentions to anyone. For you here are choices and judgments to be made. You must draw aside the many curtains (of others) of darkness and let their light shine through. You have the patience of a saint and will stay with an individual until they see the light. The very same light that warms your back gives you the tools to confront the world. You must engage the world and all its problems, even if it means losing some of your own peace and tranquility. Another hurdle you must overcome is your self-destruction of staying in any relation to fight dark and light and becoming over controlled by this individual, so much that you lose your self-esteem and self-confidence. You must in this life time become extremely independent as to control your own life and live your own life. When you are faced with an individual you must know when to give up before they have you in their control. Your weak physical points are the neck and throat area. You rarely show your temper, but when you've had enough, you've had enough and you blow, but remain friends with individuals, because they are aware you were probably correcting them to make them improve their lives and stay on their right path. You must improve your life within this life time without self destruction as you were in your past life as a Scorpio. At some time within this life or your past life, you were probably the victim of some deliberate injustice. You may have been robbed or driven out of your home. As a result, you carry feelings of anger and distrust. Fear of repeating your past life may hamper your growth in this one.

NOTES

Despite your self-destructive tendency, your social behavior is friendly and spontaneous. Though still a rebel at heart, in this lifetime you are constrained by your own anxiety. Your supernatural powers have not always been used in a positive way but, this time; these gifts will help you reach elevated levels of consciousness, as long as they are used in the service of others and more constructive goals. You must overcome your residual fears, distrust, and anger to achieve your positive nature of Taurus's Light and to appreciate the beauty and pleasures of this life. You must let the Taurus's Light push out the Scorpio darkness; this will eliminate former torments and will appease by new found peace.

NOTES

GEMINI WITH A PAST LIFE IN SAGITTARIUS

(Searching for the "There" There)

You are known as the <u>Messenger of God</u> with an association with communication of the physical world and the spiritual dimension. You are the fastest planet in the solar system you make a trip around the Sun in only 88 days. This is 104,000 mph, almost twice as fast as Earth. You are considered a speedball, quick to judge, quick to react, quick to change. Quick, as in clever and lively, but also quick, as in momentary, superficial, and passing, and must have the last word in edge wise. You also possess extraordinary powers of persuasion (Manipulative). You also contradict yourself in a fraction of a second, not because they were seduced by an interesting argument, but because a new perspective is sufficiently attractive for them to want to take credit for it. You must not just try to blend in to society, you must use the solar light, which you are the closest plant to the Sun and the greatest similarity to that star, and you must use its powers to build your communication abilities and share your vast amounts of channeled information and share it with the world. You must also distance yourself from your physical body to find your spiritual body; you are considered a cling-on. The physical body is not going to evolve, just your spiritual body does. And when you are aware and enlightened by this you will evolve spiritually. Once you have become enlightened of this action of yourself, you will proceed by dropping the split personality and your high and low attitudes. You are however, given gifts for which to use to complete your spiritual evolution, they are curiosity, creativity, friendly, multi-talented, intelligent, and open. The traits you must be-aware of is the flightiness, fickleness, impatience, restlessness, snappish, sarcastic ness, gossipy, cynical, with these negative traits you are nothing but a fast-talker, charmingly persuasive quick-witted entertainer. You are known as the double-edged sword that could cut in two very distinct and opposite ways. You a hard to catch and hard to pin down just like the mercury within a thermometer, like quicksilver, go to touch it and it scatters like a reversed magnet. During this life time you must allow people and their ideas to touch you and resist the urge to flee at the slightest emotional or intellectual discomfort. To connect with the world, you must penetrate beneath appearances creating links between ideas between you and others and ultimately, between this world and the world above. Your weak point is your heart, not just for the intimacy or love, but the heart of the ideas of others and yourself. If you make a promise you must stick to it. You must do this with organization and eagerness, not like the Sagittarian you were in your past life with a reputation of being disorganized and a spoiled child. You must realize that sharing does not restrain your freedom, it enhances it. By opening up yourself to others you will overcome the leftover self-absorption that has hindered your spiritual growth.

NOTES

CANCER WITH A PAST LIFE IN CAPRICORN

(Ever-Changing Moon)

You are known as the <u>Feminine Principle in the Universe</u>, the physical world of manifestation and finality, doubt and limitation. Within this life time you must conquer negative influences by combining positive aspects. Within this month there is less mercy in the universe, less time between cause and effect, and less time between actions and their consequences. Your planet is closest to the moon, each and every night; the Moon shows us a different face which coincides with your personality such as, your feelings of instability, uncertainty, and insecurity. First and foremost you must regain these qualities back. You must not do this within material comfort, nor by becoming cautious, apprehensive, and acquisitive, do not, I repeat, do not create a protective shell of material things to hide within an uncertain world. You are prone to depression and severe mood swings, from joy to sadness to anger and back again within seconds. You are a keen observer and quickly understand what other need or want, looking for hints of change or trouble along the way. You are also very intuitive, but also very vulnerable to absorbing other negativity, therefore you must constantly protect yourself from predators. This is one of the reasons you may retreat into a shell, hiding behind a mask of seeming indifferences. This fear of hurt could immobilize you and prevent you from taking any action that could benefit someone else or yourself. You find no comfort within the light so you try to escape the finite and apparently predetermined aspects of the physical world which are a constant worrisome companion. You usually look for negativity lurking everywhere and usually find it. You have a fear of being misjudged, and constantly seek reassurance and recognition, taken to the extremes, this anxiety can paralyze you, the future terrifies you, the past is reassuring and you recall it with great delight, you almost always enter de-`je-vue. You try to seek refuge in the past, stubbornly refusing to abandon its cocoon-like security. You must remember that limitations, finality, endings, restrictions, doubts, and death are all illusions, you must realize that seeing, hearing, smelling, touching, and tasting, are all forms of the hidden spiritual worlds, of these five senses we only use 5% of reality, by excluding 95% of reality from our awareness, we miss the underlying spiritual truth of all creations. You can improve your spiritual evolution by adopting a force of healing that connects you to the higher levels where you'll find true sharing, unity, love, and balance, than adopt the sword of power to elevate reality to a higher and purer level to see beyond the physical world to the worlds above. You must emerge from your amour of material possessions and your masks of indifferences, and expose yourself to risks, to do this you must recognize the Light of the Moon is everlasting even though it has traits of uncertain and changeable aspects. You must release your talents of empathy and intuitive understanding and share it with others for your own sake.

NOTES

By doing this, you begin to look beyond and create a genuine connection to the spiritual world. Your weak point is your fragile stomach and depression which was caused by the way you treated people in your previous life as a Capricorn who had an enormous amount of pride and was totally obsessed with professional victory, honor, and respectability. You would bolster about your own reputation and how you would take on impossible tasks only to gain admiration of others. You were appointed judge and jury and, as a consequence, condemned the mistakes committed by others. Though you saw yourself as a guardian of the moral order, you neglected morality's most important attribute, mercy. As a result you created many enemies and often considered shameless. Consumed by social missions, you were, oddly enough, oblivious to other people and the real pleasures of life such as; home, family, friends. Within this life you must learn flexibility, generosity, relationship, and parenthood. Here you will find the ultimate satisfaction and your true success

~~~~~~~~~~NOTES~~~~~~~~~~

LEO WITH A PAST LIFE IN AQUARIUS

(Breaking the Pride of Lions)

Your sign is considered one of the four Holy Entities, the other three being the bull (Taurus), the eagle, and humankind, energy descends from the Worlds Above into our world through these four entities. You receive your energy directly from the Sun and you are the only sign under its influence. Because of this, you believe that the world revolves around you. You are confident of your own power and abilities, that you broadcast your self-assurance to the whole world. When you're out in public you walk around like you're from royalty and behave somewhat omnipotent or benevolent. You demand respect or otherwise retaliate. Like queens or kings you can be arrogant and disdainful. Your weak point of the body is your heart and body; it both has been given the responsibility of pumping out and distributing all the energy you receive. You treat colleagues and friends like they are no help to you and not as equal either. You can be heavy-handed and dictatorial, like authoritarian parents who feel they are surrounded by innocent and inexperienced children. You are always looking for a kingdom to rule and flattery will buy you. You are considered one of the three most negative signs because you can give life, but you could also destroy it. As long as you remain constructive and proactive you can be an effective channel for enormous positive energy. In order to act positively, you must come to understand that you are neither the center of the universe, nor a king or queen. You were blessed with great power in order to be guides on the path to enlightenment. You were not blessed with generosity, strength, honesty, charisma, and creativity to satisfy your own ego. You do not deserve these gifts any more than a bird deserves its wings, they were given to share and care for others and to assist you to make your self-improvements. If you want to keep your privileged position, you must use your gifts selflessly and fight the delusion that your earthly gifts are the product of your own genius. Your mind is not the source of your gifts, the Light is the source, and your abilities are the blessings of the Light. The greater your abilities, the stronger your delusions.

NOTES

Pride is your culprit, because of this you go through this life facing situations where your pride is put through tests. To conquer these tests, you must not pursue honor or respect because nothing is owed to you. You must be attentive to others and open to the possibilities that others opinions may have merit. You must give help anonymously, without looking for personal benefit or glory, then and only then you will overcome your enormous pride. From your past life as an Aquarian you brought tremendous inner power, however, you were never a model of discipline, and you are still seeking originality at any cost. You are considered a rule breaker which causes others not to take you seriously. Your relationships mean the world to you but you are always afraid of abandonment. You tolerate abuse in order to maintain closeness, you let relationships dominate you, because of this, you will never develop spiritually to your potential. Within this life time you must first become independent, and not allow flattery to corner you into a dead end relationship filled with abuse. You must not let your ego trap you.

NOTES

VIRGO WITH A PAST LIFE IN PISCES

(Proud Mary)

Your sign is considered the <u>Month of Repentance</u>. Your sign has diametrically opposed energy intelligence and the highest level of consciousness. During this life time you should take advantage of the opportunities to unify rich and poor and balance their energies. You jump too hastily to a conclusion, which causes you to have very weak digestive systems. Your main characteristic is your perpetual quest for order and perfection; nothing disturbs you more than untidiness. You are reliable and responsible, and it is a point of honor for you to complete every task. Your perfectionism prevents you from grasping the bigger picture causing your views of the world reduced to a single grain of sand, when the entire beach should be taken into account. Your quest for perfection causes you to focus on the inadequacies and errors of those around you. You are seldom diplomatic or tactful, and often lack the sensitivity required for a meaningful exchange of ideas. It's not that you intend to hurt others; errors and imperfections insult your sense of order and you lash out to rectify the flaws as quickly as possible. You believe your perfect abilities authorize you to comment on and criticize others as you see fit. At the same time, however, you tend to consider yourself above reproach. With this attitude, you mimic the unassailable Virgin Mary. Although you mix easily with all classes of people, you can be almost unbearably proud. Your perceptions of reality are fragmented and only see a fraction of the whole picture. You are not very spiritual but can develop your spiritual potential by seeing beyond the physical world. You must learn to focus your critical eye on yourself and not assume that your conclusion is absolute truth. When you feel compelled to criticize or pass judgment you must ask yourself, "do I see the whole picture, or is there something I've missed?" By holding back, by restricting your initial impulse, you can escape your shortsidedness and begin to see the larger picture. You must also refrain from giving advice to others until you have questioned your own motives. More than any other improvement, you must resist passing judgment on first impressions. As I have said prior, this is the sign of Repentance, which means to examine your past life as a Pisces, consumed by your dreams, fantasies, and melodramatics' causing you to lack in discernment between right and wrong and good and bad. You had to confront numerous obstacles, you often just let things happen, when they didn't work out, you succumbed to self-pity. This same fragility emotion may have led you to seek refuge in drugs or alcohol behaviors. To make your improvement in this life you must gain more realistic and less hypersensitive view of the world. You must use more reason and less emotion in making your decisions. Self-discipline and determination will keep you grounded for own benefit and others. You must also stop your whining, this lifetime is an opportunity to settle accounts, forgive, and move on.

NOTES

SCORPIO V. TAURUS

Taurus and Scorpio have much in common. Both are months of universal negativity, yet both contain days of immense positive energy. Moreover, out of all the signs of the Zodiac, they alone have been given additional names. Scorpio has been given the names of, exactness, on target, or right on, appropriate for Scorpio's internal energy intelligence; Taurus has the distinctive pre-exilic names of, brightness, Light, which is both a challenge and its saving grace. One challenge faced by Taurus is their tendency to be placent and to feel always correct in their position. Taurus is too comfortably connected to the Light, no matter how serious or devastating their circumstances. It is quite futile for them to adapt to punishment or teach a lesson, to a Taurus who has judged you. Taurus will always feel that the truth is always on their side no matter what punishment is dished out to them. This can be a serious obstacle for those Taurus's who are not spiritually inclined. It was not by coincidence that the commencement of the role by King Solomon took place in the month of Taurus, and that its completion occurred in the month of Scorpio. These two months were carefully chosen by King Solomon to begin and end his endeavor. Make no mistake in considering that even the construction of his empire was also finished within the month of Scorpio. King Solomon, the Wise, understood the cosmos and the Gods by which to tap its power. Solomon knew that completing the empire in the month of Scorpio would provide an infusion of spiritual energy intelligence sufficient to fuel the empire for some four hundred years. In their wisdom, the sages realized that the all knowing Force must have foreseen man's greed and would race for power with their desire to receive for self alone and incapable of dealing with a large infusion of spiritual energy. Thus, he found the cosmos in a situation not unlike the situation in lunar Scorpio, which resolved itself in the great surge. In the case of Scorpio, the solution was to infuse the universe with a positive energy sufficient to restrict the unlimited needs to desire to receive. The day chosen was September 12th at sundown. A similar infusion of positive energy was necessary to stabilize the enormous negative power of Taurus. He resolved the matter departing this world on the 18th day of lunar Taurus. Yet, spiritually minded individuals are strongly advised to begin a new adventure on the 18th day of lunar Taurus, for success is all but assured. Finishing or completion of ventures should take place in the lunar month of Scorpio.

MERCURY RETROGRADE

When Mercury goes retrograde you must treat it like the spinning wheels of a vehicle, the wheels seem to be going in reverse while in actuality it's just an optical illusion. Do not listen to all those fearful stories, of while Mercury being in retrograde, everything in your life goes haywire. This is an optical illusion. So push those fears out of your subconscious mind and move forward like any other day.

NOTES

CHAPTER V

PSYCHOMETRY

Psychometry – (the measurement of the duration, force, interrelations, or other aspects of mental processes, as by psychological tests and the supposed faculty of divining knowledge about a person connected with it, through contact with the object). The theory behind the practice of psychometry is that an object that has been in the possession of a person or associated with definite incidents can absorb vibrations from the owner, and that a sensitive (a clairvoyant) can become aware of these impressions. There are speculations as the means by which this process operates. One theory is that the vibrations are of physical origin, that the sensitivity of the clairvoyant is able to receive. The second idea, the vibrations are of a spirit character received from the owner's spirit self, and these the spirit awareness of the clairvoyant is able to receive. A third explanation is that the object acts as a means of contact between the clairvoyant, the owner of the object, and your guide, and from this personal attributes and descriptions are given through the faculty of clairvoyance. In this connection it is well to consider that there can be an effect of blending or awareness of the spirit personalities between two people-a spirit consciousness of each other, in a similar way to that which we are conscious of a physical awareness. For example, when two people are attracted to each other (or repelled) this is a result of spirit affinity or spirit enmity. It may be the process known as "natural selection" arises from this, which explains why a deep bond of brotherhood or sisterhood, or love itself, comes into being between people. Psychometry may be a form of clairvoyance as between two people, in addition clairvoyant pictures and thoughts aided by the nearness of your guides who acts as the spirit communicator. In order for you to learn the way to develop this gift, he should take an object, without knowing who it belongs to, seek the state of Alpha and attune yourself with your spirit guides so that your Third-Eye can receive impressions. When these are received you should then speak or write, and describe the impression in total detail, either thoughts or pictures. You must not allow your own personal thoughts or impressions to add to what your mind has received. You must not be discouraged on the first attempt, if you do not get a message accepted by the owner of the article, you will, just have patience and try again. In all forms of being a psychic, it is practice that makes you perfect, the working is the gift. Certain people have a kind of "sixth sense" that allows them to pick up these hidden vibrations and impressions, and bring them into their waking consciousness. Such people are called "Psychometrists". Just remember psychometry is seeing through touch. Have you ever borrowed something and when you touched it you felt a positive energy or a negative one? People's personal possessions absorb their energies and when you touch, the object releases this energy into your hands.

NOTES

Again psychometry is "seeing" through touch; remember everything is pure energy, from your favorite jewelry clothing, even just a business card. These are tools for psychics; this is an excellent way to train your abilities. With psychometry, you can reach past your normal five senses. Everything leaves a polarity imprint whether positive or negative.

STEPS IN PRESENTING EVIDENCE

- *You will need a pen and included journal when you first start developing.*
- *Always place yourself into a meditative state of consciousness.*
- *Place object either in hands or unto your third eye.*
- *Direct your power to pay concentrated and consciously directed attention to the impressions that are aroused in your minds eye through the actions of your senses. This directed and concentrated attention means that it is necessary to develop the ability to keep your attention fixed on any part of the object at will.*
- *Really feel the object, (at first for a good ½ hour if needed and jot down everything from your senses.*
- *What feelings are you getting?*
- *How does the object feel, (hot, cold, tingly, or vibrating)?*
- *Did you smell anything, (flowers, body odors, oil, grease, etc…)?*
- *Did you taste anything, (sweet, bitter, wood, metals, etc…)?*
- *Did you hear anything, (words, voices, music, animals, buzzing, etc…)?*
- *Last but not least, what did you see within your third-eye?*

After you have trained yourself to have confidence in what you sensed, you will delete the pen and paper, the time will decrease in half and you will pinpoint the finer points of identification such as:

- *Estimated height and build of person*
- *Outstanding peculiarities such as artificial limbs or deformities.*
- *Clothing, style and color.*
- *Quick detail descriptions of facial features.*
- *Mannerisms*

Take time to scan the body, this is very important because by doing so and if the person is deceased, this technique will lead to the practice of mediumship and healing.

NOTES

DREAMS

Dream state is our time to communicate with our loved ones and spirit guides. Loved ones or spirit guides, most of the time gives us symbols to work with. To assist you with these symbols I will give you a brief list of symbols and their meanings. To further yourself in your translation of your dreams I suggest purchasing a dream dictionary for a reference guide. The soul never thinks without a mental picture. Listed below are Universal Symbols, A to Z.

Symbol	Meaning
Abundance	desire for independence
Accident	something unplanned
Actor/Actress	desire for recognition
Adultery	guilt
Alter	self-sacrifice
Anchor	stability, desire a permanent home
Animal	feelings, afraid or welcoming
Apple	desires
Arrow	pleasure, festivity
Auction	promise of abundance
Baby	crying/ frustrated, laughing/ fulfillment, sleeping/ wait
Balloon	frustration
Basement	a place of refuge or retreat
Bathroom	elimination of undesired
Battle	internal conflict
Bedroom	rest and recovery
Bells	fulfillment and joy
Bicycle	hard work brings plans to fruition
Birds	one state of being to another
Birth	new phase, or new aspect of self
Black Horse	change of fortunes
Blue	tranquility, understanding
Bridge	overcome difficulties, a change
Broom	ability to clean up a situation
Brown	patients, truth, sincerity
Bull	animal nature, stubbornness
Burial	end of a phase, new direction

NOTES

Candle	constancy
Cane/Crutch	need of support
Capital	unbalanced heart center
Castle	ambition
Cave	need for solitude
Circle	perfection, infinity
Cities	gathering of consciousness
Climbing	self-mastery process
Clock	passage of time, need action
Clothes	attitude, personality
Coffin	trapped, obstacles
Cradle	potential for advancement
Crossing a River	fundamental change of attitude
Crying	why, for a happy or sad outcome
Crystal	union of matter and spirit
Curtains	concealment
Darkness	subconscious turning inward
Death	end of something, new opportunities
Dog	loyalty, laziness, anger
Eating	need for new interests
Eight	dissolution, separation
Even Numbers	balance and harmony
Evening	descending into subconscious world
Eye	perception, self-examination
Falling	failing to live up to expectations
Fire	anger, purification, abundant energy
Five	expansion, change, understanding justice
Flowers	contentment, pleasure
Flying	you raise higher
Four	too materialistic, law, physical power

NOTES

Girl	your showing too much immaturity
Glass	being able to see into future
Graduation	completing a phase
Green	finance, fertility, luck, energy, growth
Hair	thoughts, gray hair wise thoughts
Hammer	power to drive forward
Helpful Animal	the instinctive self
Highway	on your right path, the way ahead
House	personality and conscious interests from a spiritual view
Ice	coldness of character, frigidity, rigidity
Illness	boredom, delays
Indigo	impulsiveness, depression, ambition,
Jail	confinement, frustration, inability to act
Judge/Jury	your own conscious
Key	the answer to a problem
Kiss	satisfaction, completion
Ladder	ability to climb up to success
Left	your subconscious side, logical side
Light	hope, renewed faith
Lock	security frustration
Man/Male	age indicates maturity or lack of it
Mask	falsehood, deception, concealment
Mirror	re-examine yourself
Mother	haven, comfortable, feeling nurtured
Nakedness	real, truth, exposed, natural
Night	your greatest strength in your super consciousness
Nine	rebirth, intuition, travel, karma,
Noon	your greatest clarity of consciousness
Ocean	opportunity, spirituality
Odd Numbers	imbalance and discord
One	the source, the beginning, the ego
Orange	encouragement, adaptability, attraction, kindness
Owl	wisdom, need of further evaluation
Pearl	joy, broken means misunderstandings
Pirate	suspicion
Pyramid	thirst for knowledge, seeking

NOTES

Railroad	*set a path to follow*
Rainbow	*great happiness, opportunity*
Reading	*learning, gaining in knowledge, perceiving*
Red	*strength, health, vigor, danger, charity*
Right	*your conscious, correctness, the artistic side*
Ring	*completion, continuity, loyalty*
River	*spirituality, a boundary*
Rocks	*the unchanging self*
Rodents	*a less than nice person, distrust, betrayal*
Roller Skates	*more effort*
Roses	*yellow- friendship*
	pink- love
	red- compassion
	white- wedding
Ruins	*failure of plans*
Sacrifice	*overcoming pride*
School	*a need to learn*
Scissors	*distrust*
Sea	*stormy periods, calm periods*
Seven	*endurance, evolution, wisdom*
Shadow	*instability*
Six	*cooperation and balance*
Skeleton	*the basics, the root of a problem*
Snake	*spiritual wisdom, a state*
Snake-Bite	*infusion of wisdom*
Soldiers	*force, power*
Spade	*penetrating, cutting, tough work ahead*
Sunrise	*awakening of consciousness*
Sunset	*need to protect assets*
Swan	*beauty, comfort, satisfied*
Sword	*conflict*
Telescope	*the need to get closer to someone*
Thief	*loss or fear of loss, insecurities*
Three	*past, present, future, completion*
Thunder	*deep anger*

NOTES

Touching	norm, lying on of hands
Trains	forceful and direct,
Traveling	the act of spiritual advancement
Tree	life principle, psychic growth, success
Tunnel	hiding, afraid
Turning	changing, developing
Twins	ego and alter ego
Two	duality, positive and negative
Umbrella	shelter, protecting one-self
Veil	enlightenment
Violet	tension, power, sadness, sentimental
Volcano	expect exploded emotions
Wall	cautious, proceed with caution
Water	humble spiritually
Wedding	creating plans, happiness, success
White Horse	symbol of life
Wild Horse	uncontrolled instinctive urges
Winged Horse	going to the light
Witch	supernatural ability, wisdom
Woman	age indicates maturity or lack of it
Wreath	self-pity
Yellow	persuasion, charm, confident, jealousy, joy, comfort
Zero	the universe, infinity, the all

NOTES

TYPES OF DREAMS

<u>Ordinary dreams</u> are based on activities of the unconscious in response to what we have seen or heard in your waking hours. The unconscious stores knowledge that has made an impression that remains filed in the brain and unperceived until "read" by dream symbols, which is the language of the soul.

<u>Lucid dreams</u> are dreams that you can control because you are aware that you are dreaming. You can also decide what to dream before going to sleep and then dream about the very thing that you planned to.

<u>Telepathic dreams</u> know the language of the Angels, allowing the dead and living to speak in dreamland. A mental communication can also occur, mind-to-mind between two people.

<u>Premonitory dreams</u> are when your spirit body leaves your physical body and ventures on a voyage of discovery. These dreams reveal the future and allow the dreamer to see truths that are not accessible in waking life. These dreams also detect information about an imminent event. Dreams are a catalyst that sets your body into motion to follow and fulfill your wishes and desires.

<u>Nightmares</u> are linked to early childhood, when we are inexperienced, usually before the age of three, when we have not developed a sense of conscious and right or wrong. Nightmares are usually a warning of your doing something incorrect or others are causing an injustice toward you.

NOTES

<u>*Recurring dreams*</u> *releases repressed emotions and focuses our attention on unresolved problems. Their aim is to restore our personality back to its complete state. These are some common recurring dreams:*

- *Being chased is a sign of anxiety and a lack of confidence.*

- *Being naked in public is difficulty in being yourself.*

- *Climbing means a desire to make it to the top.*

- *Dining with Celebrities is an urge to gain admittance to a higher society.*

- *Falling means being afraid of a moral decline, but expect good fortune if you fall without being hurt.*

- *Flying is a longing for freedom and a wish to escape restraints.*

- *Meetings means that the person is in the back of your mind, whether he/she is alive or deceased.*

- *Meeting with the deceased and is a real vivid meeting, seeing that persons spirit is alive and well means this person has had a loving influence in your life and will keep giving you help by meeting in your dreams.*

- *Meetings with strangers means if it is a woman this represents your intuition, if it is a male this represents your strength.*

- *Missing a train or plane, this unveils a frustration at being unable to find your vocation or path in life.*

NOTES

YOUR REMARKABLE BRAIN

Before you start you must realize you do have to use both sides of your brain. You will want a brain that thinks clearly, works quickly, and concentrates intently throughout your years. You also want an agile mind capable of storing and processing a large amount of information. We recognize there is room for improvement where our cognitive capabilities are concerned. This is a tool for boosting your brain health immediately. Your brain weighs only three pounds and is the size of your two fists pressed together. Your brain is seventy-eight percent water, ten percent fat, and eight percent protein, and has the consistency of soft tofu. Each half of your brain, right and left, controls the opposite side of your body. Your left side controls logic, analyzing, objectives (determining real and actual). Your right side controls intuition, creativity, and is subjective (your temperament and judgment). Your frontal lobe controls planning, movement, and speech. Your temporal lobe controls hearing and memory. Your parietal lobe controls pain, touch sensation, as well as spatial orientation (living in the now). Your occipital lobe controls vision, while your cerebellum controls balance, coordination, and movement. Finally your brain stem transmits messages to and from the spinal cord, and regulates automatic body function like breathing, blood pressure, and heart rhythm. All of your brain functions are regulated through meditation daily. Meditation is simply focused attention, directed breathing, words or phrases (known as mantra,) or mental images. By drawing your attention to one place, you're also taking your focus away from anxious thoughts and mental chatter. Meditation quiets the mind, slows down your brains deterioration relating to aging. Both guided imagery and self hypnosis promotes relaxation. A basic approach is to imagine an actual place from your past where you experienced and felt extremely happy, secure, and peaceful. Then picture yourself in that scene, making all your sense impressions as sharp as possible. While in meditative state, gently and consciously tighten one muscle group at a time, following by releasing this tension. You progressively move from head to toe or from toe to head upward. The idea is to pay attention to how your body feels as you alternately squeeze and relax each major muscle group. When you are finished you'll feel relaxed all over. Now your memory works by filing information away into your memory. When you are awake, your senses are bombarded with stimuli (activity), such as sights, sounds, and other sensations that are all potential memories. These than pass through your immediate memory into a holding area called the short-term-memory. Only a slight percentage of information makes its way to the holding area called your long-term-memory. In short-term includes information such as names, what you ate for breakfast. When you have trouble remembering something, it is often because you were distracted. Here is a basic memory training technique:

NOTES

> *Focus* your attention, especially when new information is being presented to you. Consciously absorb all details and meanings from your source without being distracted. Take several items frequently used daily and place them on a table. Stare at them, one at a time, paying close attention to details never noticed before. Your brain is like a sponge so you will notice quite a few details.

> *Create* a mental snapshot or visual image of the information. When you observe the items from above and before going to the next object, take a mental snapshot of the item in full detail, the details you were aware of and the details that are new to you. Notice the length of the new information from each item, the information should have quadrupled.

> *Link* the visual images in a coherent and meaningful way. These techniques are the key to build up memories when you want to recall them later. The ideas or images become part of a chain, starting from the first item, which is associated with the second, and so on. From the items above, connect all the items together and try to make a story with them. This is your link to memory.

NOTES

WHO'S LOOKING BACK?

Do me a favor; take a look at yourself in the mirror. Who's looking back? Someone having a bad hair day or a zit attack? Look a little closer. Who's there now? Now one more time, look really, really closely. Do you see someone who angers quickly? Someone getting a divorce? Or a promotion for a job well done? Look even closer, not turning inside out. What if you woke up one morning, and you had no reflection? Not in anything you gaze into, none anywhere? Who would you be then? Your own concept of yourself would be determined strictly by emotion and self-exploration. So, unless you get someone to draw a picture of you, you wouldn't have that magic mirror telling you more about yourself than you probably need to know. Not seeing ourselves physically could possibly open new rapport with others. Think about it. Only your best friends would tell you if you have mustard on your chin or snot on your upper lip, but if we always had to depend on others to tell us these things, then maybe there would be fewer strangers in the world; a community of neighbors helping each other with grooming deficiencies. But then again, that's just part of this perfect little imagery world where people are judged by their sneakers, and not by their characters. I guess what I'm really asking is, does the mirror really just the plaything of humanity's vanity? Though mirrors do keep us looking our best, they tend to play a serious role in other aspects of life as well. For example, in ancient times, mirrors were considered a tool of mysteries. We haven't strayed to far from this today. Enoptromancy (mirror scrying) is still a respected form of divination today. Mirrors have been used over the ages for a myriad of reasons. Doctors once held mirrors under the noses of terminally ill patients to check for breathing. Mirrors are an elegant choice of decoration. When it comes to omens, breaking a mirror stands with the unforgivable. We are thus sentenced to seven agonizing years of bad luck-yikes! But on the other hand, Feng Shui practioners will tell you that mirrors can add good luck if hung appropriately. This does not apply to sectional mirrors, they must be one piece, preferably round, and hung high enough so as not to cut off the head of the tallest person in the room. People waiting in line don't seem to mind waiting if there is a mirror on the wall where they can see their reflection. I believe the psychological reason for this doesn't have anything to do with vanity, but security and freedom, to actually see more of their surroundings and the feeling of not being trapped in a long snail-paced line. Mirrors are used for illusions, especially when added to a wall to make a room appear larger. A mirror in a waiting room would serve two purposes. One, they can occupy their minds by concentrating on themselves. Two, the mirror gives out a timeless energy. Is it possible that mirrors hold magical appeal because they reflect light? After all, light reflection is the source of our visions, both physically and mentally. We not only see the world around us, but with the help of these light-reflecting mirrors, we see into the other side as well. Let's face it; mirrors are a pure form of magic. Now look in the mirror again, and just imagine. Mirror, mirror on the walls, other side calls?

NOTES

THE PENDULUM

SWINGING TO SUCCESS

The pendulum is a simple, accurate and versatile device consisting of a weight attached to a chain or thread. Arguably the most underrated item in the magician's arsenal, the pendulum can reveal information not found any other way. It can read energy, patterns, extracting information from deep within your subconscious. You must obtain a pendulum and use it daily for self-improvement and psychic development. If you can't afford an actual pendulum, tie a ring to a piece of thread; use a necklace that is looped through a heavy charm. There are two ways to read your pendulum. First is if it spins in a clockwise pattern, this means yes, counter-clockwise, is no, if it stands still, it does not want to answer right now, wait a little while and try to ask the same question, it should respond the second time. The second way to read your pendulum is if it swings left to right, this means yes, or to and from you, this means no. It's all in the way you train it. Yes, train it, start with telling it while spinning clockwise or left to right, this means yes. Then train it for your no answer. The pendulum can also locate lost items, or used with a quija board for communication with your spirit guides and deceased loved ones, however, be very careful while using the quija board, you don't want to access any dark energy. Always place four amethysts at each corner of your board for protection.

NOTES

CHAPTER VI

BEHIND 101

101 is for you to become more attuned daily through guided meditation, contemplate daily on something other than the dogma of society, doing your spells daily will teach you how to send out what you want into the ether. Being repetitive in your practices will bring you to a point to where you will not need to do spells anymore, you'll just think and send. Never ever forget what you do, always write it down and always ask the Divine Spirit that it be done correctly and for the good of all!!! This section is a guide of information to assist you on your way to spiritual growth. The definition of magic is "change" to be a change in consciousness, example; let say you do a magical spell to get fifty dollars. It is your "will" to get the money. You go out for a walk, and although when walking it is your habit to go right at a particular corner, something inspires you to take a left instead. A block down the street you meet an old friend who returns fifty dollars you had loaned him several years ago. So what made you turn left? Your act caused change in the physical world resulting in you turning left. Perhaps it was a sound, sight, or Divine, telling you to turn left. Everything you do is a magical act. It occurs in conformity with will, using means not currently understood by traditional science, magic is not supernatural. If our entire universe came about by either a creation of Intelligent Design, or merely as the result of chance events, we must still come to the conclusion; everything in the universe is natural. In the old days, magic was considered deep occult secrets, today, many of these occult secrets are taught to children before they enter school. In a sense, you are now a scientist of the future. That is why you should follow "a scientific method"; this method controls all variables in experiments and keeps accurate records of these experiments. This is why I stress so firmly, for you to keep a journal for everything you do.

NOTES

In the old days, society believed that people who tampered with true magic, whether good or evil, had no morality. Yet, true magic is usually far more moral with people who use it more than those who do not, especially those professing to be highly moral. It is because with true magic you must obey all natural laws that involve working with karma. In magic you are free to choose what you want to do, whatever you desire, however, true magic will invariably choose the path of Light, called morally correct. When you choose the path of Dark that is not for moral purposes the effect from this type of magic will come back to three-fold. Such is the universal Law of Karma. In true magic there is no such thing as white, green, gray, or black magic, there is only magic period, because you are aware and understand the Law of Karma. You should always avoid black magic, yes; there are black magicians, because they do not understand the functions and fundamentals of the Law of Karma. Suicide would give you a karma debt from a result of your action, also helping one to do so because of a chronic illness (ex. Dr. Kevorkian, Dr. of death) will result in a karma debt for you. Everyone must walk their path completely without executing life before its time. If you're in question as to helping someone, ask your Spirit Guides, or go straight to the Divine Source to see if you should get involved. You receive your rewards and debts within this lifetime, however, any remnants leftover, will be brought through in your next incarnation. Each life is a case of experiencing all things, just one at a time with each life you live. It is these experiences that keep you on your correct path. I will give a brief description of each type of magic to familiarize you with the correct way and the incorrect way in performing magic.

NOTES

BLACK is the science and art of causing change to occur in conformity with will for the purpose of causing either physical or non-physical harm to yourself or others, it is done consciously or unconsciously. Put out good and you will receive good. Put out evil, even unintentionally, and evil is what you will get. Such is the Law! However, evil is a tool in which to learn from, and almost everyone uses at first because it is enticing, this would be unintentional evil mind. Just remember the old saying; practice makes perfect. This would be the point when you go from dark to light, when you become aware that the dark side doesn't really work, because it always comes back. Through personal trials and errors, I've grown toward the light side of magic. It does take time, but eventually we all take notice to this fact.

GRAY is the science and art of causing change to occur in conformity and will for the purpose of causing either physical or non-physical harm to yourself or others, and is done consciously or unconsciously without the sadistic acts of the black art but more maliciously.

GREEN is the science and art of causing change to occur in conformity and will for the purpose maintaining the Earth and all living things within, without malice or evil, using of the earth for a holistic approach.

WHITE is the science and art of causing change to occur in conformity with will, using means for the purpose of obtaining knowledge and conversations with your Spirit Guides, Guardian Angels, Divine Source, and your higher self.

Here are your five steps you need to apply daily to take you on the right road to the Divine source:

1. *Consistency is living with the Divine Source everyday.*
2. *Meditation quiets the soul for you to learn.*
3. *Contemplation increases knowledge.*
4. *Intention is thoughts are things; make sure it's always positive.*
5. *Action puts you out there through thought to receive what you want.*

NOTES

WAXING AND WANING LUNAR *PHASES*

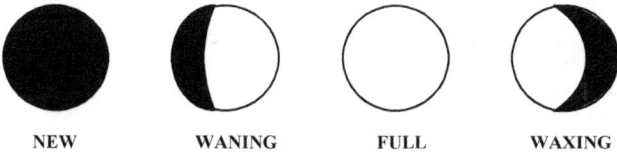

NEW　　　WANING　　　FULL　　　WAXING

Two main phases are as follows: the time from the New Moon, through the First Quarter, to the Full Moon is known as the Waxing Moon. From the Full Moon through the Last Quarter, to the New Moon is known as the Waning Moon. Constructive magic for growth is done during the <u>Waxing Cycle</u> and magic for destruction is done during the <u>Waning Cycle.</u> Constructive magic consist of: Love, Success, Protection, Health, and Fertility. Destructive magic consist of: Binding spells, Separation, Elimination, and Extermination. There is a certain element of sympathetic magic just in this time of working. For example: as the Moon grows, so grows the opportunity or as the Moon dwindles, so declines the negative power over you. I recommend initiating your spells after six o'clock at night, between the <u>Waxing</u> and the <u>Full</u> Moons; this is the most positive aspects the Moon cycles. I recommend avoiding spell work during the Waning to the New Moons; this is too negative and is a perfect time for you to rest. You will find the day of correspondence and color of your candles, located in the front of the book along with your secret alphabet, needed to decode the chants for each spell. Like I have said earlier, I'm not trying to make it difficult for you to accomplish these task or to become a Witch, I'm merely requiring and training you to work with both sides of your brain to have the ultimate effect for what you want!. Always meditate daily before applying yourself in this manual, remember your five steps!

NOTES

DAY 1 / SUNDAY / LAVENDER

Contemplation: Isis is the goddess of Earth and Sky, "the dutiful wife," "the grieving widow," "the protector of the dead." She was the counter part to the God Osiris and his guardian. She was an enchantress and a goddess of magic. Most of all, she was a teacher of the healing arts, balm, and medicine, working along side to Troth. She was the goddess of the pyramids in Egypt. Isis obtained the most secret name of Ra, the great Egyptian Sun God, so that she might use it to make herself a goddess. She fashioned a serpent from the spittle of Ra, and the earth on which it fell, and laid it in his path so it bit him. Ra cried for help from the children of the Gods with healing words and understanding lips, whose power reaches to the heavens. Isis came with her craft, whose mouth is full of the breath of life, whose spells chase pain away, and whose words make the dead live. Ra told her how he was bitten while walking and Isis said, "Tell me thy name, Divine Father, for the man shall live who is called by this name". Ra told her many of the names by which he was known, all the time growing weaker. Isis refused to heal him, repeating, "That was not thy name that you shall speak unto me. Tell it to me, which the poison may depart; for he shall live whose name is named". Finally, Ra gave Isis his true name and she caused the poison to flow away; and she became "the Queen of the Gods, she who knows Ra and his true name. Isis wanted equality along with respect of her powers, however, this is an example of black magic. In ancient myth, Ra emerged from primordial chaos at the beginning of time. Egyptian legend sometimes refers to Ra as (AMUN-RA). The word "Amun" is linked with the Egyptian word for Sun, while Ra symbolizes his qualities as endless vitality, enduring strength, and immortality. His name is also linked with the word "phrah", or pharaoh or King. Each pharaoh after Ra's reign, called themselves "Son of Ra". When ever the Queen became pregnant, she and the court believed it was Ra who impregnated her.

NOTES

KEY SPELL

Obtain a skeleton key, light some lavender candles. Tie lavender ribbon and attach key to your daily keychain for protection and chant:

NOTES

DAY 2 / MONDAY / YELLOW

Contemplation: Clearing harmful energies consist of out with the old in with the new. Go through your physical mess. Clear away things you have no use for anymore. Ask yourself why are you holding on to these things? Today find at least three things in this clutter that have some value, but that you do not regularly. These things you should give away. Do not throw them away. Once you have done this you should notice a difference in the energy before and after cleansing your space. Before you can bless your home and renew its energies, it is good spiritual practice to clear out any harmful or destructive energy forms. Energy moves naturally in waves and patterns, and often we block the free flow of energy in enclosed spaces and clutter, closed doors, a lack of ventilation, obstructed light, and we evoke a generally chaotic feel of haphazard placement of our belongings. When we block the free flow of energy in our home, it becomes stagnant, unhealthy, and un-prosperous. Out with the old and in with the new.

DREAM SPELL

Run a bath with Lavender oil, light some yellow candles; soak in the tub and reflect on all the joys and difficulties for the past year. When you are finished with your bath, allow the tub to drain, visualizing all those negative difficulties going down the drain. Before going to bed, dab some lavender oil on your pillow and chant:

NOTES

DAY 3 / TUESDAY / RED

Contemplation: Giving by listening by choosing an hour during your day to listen deeply to someone else without commenting about your own life or interests. Simply listen with full attention to the details of the speaker's world. Repeat back in your own words the information you have heard to demonstrate to the speaker that you have heard what he or she had to say. Next, give of your time for one hour today; donate your time to some charitable cause. It is natural to resist the process of giving of your time, especially since your time is a commodity that can be wasted. When you deeply consider the arrangements of this existence, what else do we truly have in each moment except time and each other? To finish this day, Give of your energy for one hour today, put your full energy into some task that does not benefit you personally. Perhaps preparing some food that someone else would enjoy or perhaps finishing someone else's tasks whose help is needed. Maybe you can offer one of your healing techniques. As you prepare to engage in these tasks, notice and write what resistance you faced, by doing this you will make yourself aware of what type of selfishness is needed to be deleted from your personality.

NO EVIL IN SPELL

Light red candles and obtain a handful of whole mustard seed at a health food store. Pour it into a bowl and let it stand by your bedside overnight. The next night, sprinkle the mustard outside the door of your home and chant:

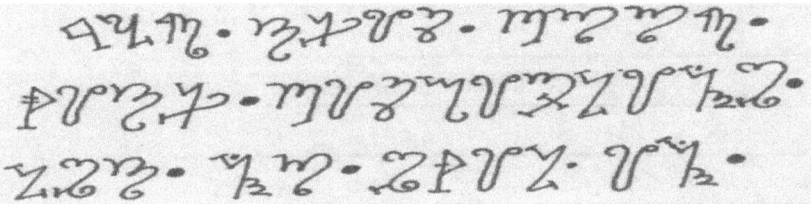

NOTES

DAY 4 / WEDNESDAY / BLUE

Contemplation: The Hermetic Principles are a branch of occult studies reputedly founded by the ancient Egyptian philosopher Hermes Trismegistus. The myth of Trismegistus is that he allegedly lived when the race of humans was still young spiritually. Hermeticism focuses on the magical workings of nature as it manifests through these seven spiritual principles:

1. <u>*Natural Law of Materialism*</u>*(The All is Mind, the Universe is Mental)*

2. <u>*Natural Law of Correspondence*</u>*(As Above so Below, As Below so Above)*

3. <u>*Natural Law of Vibration*</u>*(Nothing is at rest, everything moves, everything vibrates)*

4. <u>*Natural Law of Polarity*</u>*(Everything is Dual, everything has poles, and everything has its pair of opposites, like and unlike are the same, opposites are identical in nature, but different in degree, extremes meet, all truths are but half truths, and all paradoxes may be reconciled)*

5. <u>*Natural Law of Rhythm*</u>*(Everything flows, in and out, everything has its tides, all things rise and fall, the pendulum-swing manifests in everything, the measure of the swing to the left is the measure of the swing to the right, rhythm (compensates)*

6. <u>*Natural Law of Cause and Effect*</u>*(Every Cause has its Effect, every Effect has Its Cause, Everything happens according to Law, Chance is but a name for Law not recognized, there are many planes of causation, but nothing escapes the Law)*

7. <u>*Natural Law of Gender*</u>*(Gender is in everything, everything has its Masculine and Feminine Principles, Gender manifests on all plan*

NOTES

SPIN SPELL

Use your pendulum, light blue candles, and ask a yes or no question. You will receive your answer by the swing, chant:

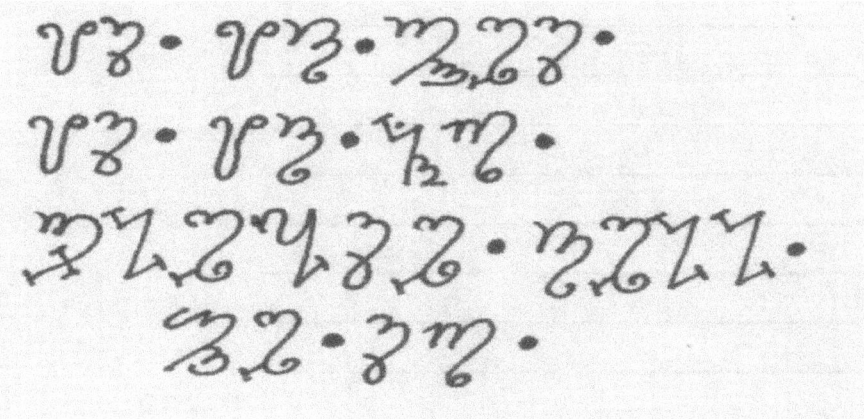

NOTES

DAY 5 / THURSDAY / GREEN

Contemplation: For the purpose of convenience of thought and study, the Hermetic Philosophy has divided the Universe into the Three Great Planes: The Great Physical Plane, the Great Mental Plane, and the Great Spiritual Plane. All of the three divisions are ascending degrees of the great scale of Life, the lowest is the undifferentiated Matter, and the highest is that of Spirit. The different Planes shade into each other so that no division may be made between the higher phenomena of the Physical and the lower of the Mental, or between the higher of the Mental and the lower of the Physical. A Plane is not a place, nor ordinary dimension of space, but more than a state or condition. It is considered that the state or condition is a degree of dimension in a scale subject to measurement. It is a Paradox, definition: (a statement contrary to common belief, a statement that seems contradictory, unbelievable, or absurd but that may be actually true in fact, a statement that is self-contradictory in fact, hence, false, a person, situation, act, etc. that seems to have contradictory or inconsistence qualities.) The Three Great Planes are regarded as three groups of degrees of Life Manifestation. The Three Great Planes are not actual divisions of the phenomena of the Universe, but terms used for thought and study of the various degrees and forms of universal activity and life. The atom of matter, the unit of force, the mind of man, and the being of the arch-angel are all but degrees in one scale, and all fundamentally the same, the difference between matter and degree and the rate of vibration, all are creations of THE ALL, and exist within the Infinite Mind of THE ALL! Within the Three Great Planes there is a division of seven minor planes.

NOTES

WISHBONE SPELL

Take a wishbone from a bird you just feasted on, light green candles and make a wish for the money, spin once clockwise and ask for this to come true this year, and then chant:

NOTES

DAY 6 / FRIDAY / PINK

Contemplation: Within the <u>Great Physical Plane</u> these seven minor places relate to physics, material things, forces, and manifestations, including all forms we call Matter, Energy, or Force:

1. <u>The Plane of Matter (A)</u> *consisting of solids, liquids, and gases.*

2. <u>The Plane of Matter (B)</u> *consisting of Matter of existence Radiant Matter, (radium)*

3. <u>The Plane of Matter ©</u> *consists of slight and vague Matter*

4. <u>The Plane of Ethereal Substance</u>, *consist of what science calls the Ether, (a substance of extreme tenuity and elasticity, pervading all universal space and acting mediums use for transmission of waves of energy, such as light, heat, electricity, etc. this Ethereal Substance is the link between Matter and Energy, and partakes of the nature in each).*

5. <u>The Plane of Energy (A)</u> *consists of forms of Energy known to science, divided into seven sub-planes: Heat, Light, Magnetism, Electricity, Attraction, Gravitation, Cohesion, And Chemical Affinity.*

6. <u>The Plane of Energy (B)</u> *consist of seven sub-planes of higher forms not yet discovered by science and are called Nature's Finer Forces, which are called upon for operations of certain forms of mental manifestations when such phenomenon becomes* possible.

7. <u>The Plane of Energy ©</u> *consist also of seven sub-planes of energy so highly advanced and only available to the beings of the Spiritual Plane. It is considered the Divine Power, almost as close as the Divine Source.*

NOTES

GARLAND LOVE SPELL

String cranberries on a 7" pink thread, light several pink candles, and drink a glass of blush wine. Place the garland on your left wrist, wear for the day and chant:

[magical script / sigils]

NOTES

DAY 7 / SATURDAY / BROWN

Contemplation: The Great Mental Plane and its seven planes

1. <u>The Plane of Mineral Mind</u> *consist of states and conditions, units of entities, groups, and combinations of the same, which animates the forms known to us as, minerals, chemicals, etc. which is considered living energy because it is of the highest Physical Plane.*

2. <u>The Plane of Elemental Mind (A)</u> *consist of mineral and chemical entities, but also comprising of the entities of the plant kingdom, they are degrees of mental and vital development and are invisible to the ordinary senses of man.*

3. <u>The Plane of Plant Mind</u>, *consists of seven sub-divisions, all regarding the Mind and Life in Plants. Plants have life, mind and "souls," as well as animals and man.*

4. <u>The Plane of Elemental Mind (B)</u> *consists of all of the Laws of Nature.*

5. <u>The Plane of Animal Mind</u> *in its seven sub-divisions equal to the sub-divisions of the Plane of Plant Mind.*

6. <u>The Plane of Elemental Mind</u> © *consists of entities invisible to the naked eye partaking in the nature of both animal and human life combining the highest forms of semi-human intelligence.*

7. <u>The Plane of Human Mind</u> *consists of seven sub-divisions, mentality, the average man occupies only the Fourth Sub-Division of mental development and only the most intelligent have crossed over into the Fifth Sub-Division. It has taken millions of years to reach this stage, and will take many more for humans to move into the Sixth and Seventh Sub-Divisions. Our own race is Fifth with stragglers from the Fourth, which has set foot upon their right path. Some of the more spiritually developed human has already proceeded into the Sixth Division known as Blue Ray Children, forerunners for the Rainbow, indigo, crystal children of today.*

NOTES

WITCHES LADDER SPELL

Cut 7 ½" of brown cord, light brown candles. Tie a knot every inch making a wish for each knot, 7 in all, when done, Carry with you for good luck, chant three times:

NOTES

DAY 8 / SUNDAY / LAVENDER

Contemplation: The Great Spiritual Plane consist of Ether, the root principle of all manifestations both Spiritual and Material Worlds. Ether is the container and foundations for all Laws of Nature and all cosmic manifestations, and is the Eternal Parent Space itself. Ether will remain as it is throughout existence. This Great Spiritual Plane has seven sub-planes within itself which entails the sevenfold nature, everything, and seven within seven within seven and so on. Within each Great Plane, consist of 7 X 7 = 49 different Planes. Each significant in its own nature and form and all of total importance, which I'll go over in the next couple of your days.

SPIRIT MESSAGE SPELL

Light lavender candles, gaze into the flame, meditate and let your mind open up to the messages. The unconscious brain will receive the messages. Thank your Spirit guides and chant:

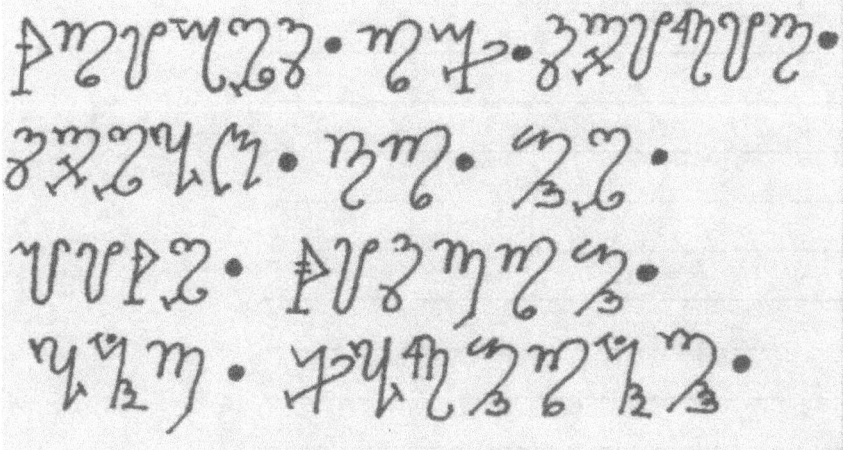

NOTES

DAY 9 / MONDAY / YELLOW

Contemplation on the 7 x 7 Planes

<u>*1. Divine Plane*</u>:

- *Avatar:* The highest Spiritual attained people with complete fulfillment, permanent death of Ego, and unity with the All.
- *Mystic:* Departing of the physical body, one with the Cosmos, and complete knowing.
- *Disciple:* Emotional induces you to rearrange and expand your mental awareness.
- *Inclined:* Intuitive sense and your awareness of your Third-Eye.
- *Believer:* First stages of awareness but questionable and cautious.
- *Primitive:* Lack of knowledge, commonsense, or a very slow mentality.
- *Atheist:* Total absence of Spiritual awareness believing only mechanical with no passion or order to the universe. One who is caught in a Biological Machine with no absolute trust.

BLESS HOME SPELL

Light some yellow candles in each room of your house. With a lit smudge stick, go around your home in a clockwise direction, hitting closets, doorways, windows. After you smudge, open all you windows for five minutes and light frankincense, then close the windows and chant three times:

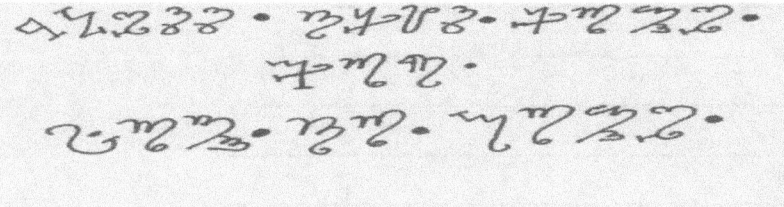

NOTES

DAY 10 / TUESDAY / RED

Contemplation on these 7 X 7 Planes, they are extraordinary you will be enlightened to know where you actually existed and where you are today.

2. <u>Monadic Plane</u>:

<u>Etheric or Borean Root Race</u> *consists not entirely physical, Beings of a higher physical etheric density, not like humanity of today and are beings of the Red Ray.*

<u>Hyperborean Root Race</u> *or the Orange Ray Beings are traces of the Borean Root Race, which have long since vanished.*

<u>Lumurian Root Race</u> *brought down by the Yellow Ray, which started activity, development, and individual free will was the mythical "Garden of Eden," which humanity "fell" from. Lumurians were over 12 feet tall and the first to develop separate genders. The Lumurian continent was located in the Pacific Ocean, known as Easter Island.*

<u>Atlantian Root Race</u> *existed years ago, again different from humanity of today. Many Atlantians had blue skin and are from the Emerald Ray, and was characterized by emotion with a result of certain periods of peacefulness and spirituality, while other periods resulting in periods of strife and occult conflicts. This went on until the break-up and sinking of the atlantian continent which is believed to be located at the base of the Rock of Gibraltar or the "Pillar of Hercules," located on the southwestern tip of Europe on the Iberian Peninsula. There are some who believe that the real Atlantis is located in the middle of the Bermuda Triangle, because of the underwater stone formation found to be about 15,000 to 20,000 years old. This continent originally filled the Atlantic Ocean. It was the longest civilization there has ever been, a divine experiment to see if people could live in a physical body and still keep their divine connection. Throughout this period, tests were set up in a number of different ways, but these humans were inevitably terminated as humans because of the use their free will to move deeper into materialism and negativity.*

NOTES

By the fifth experiment only five islands remained in a chain down to North America, of these only the mountain tips in Bermuda are exposed, the Canary Islands and the Azores can still be seen. However, when the conditions were reset in 20,000 BC for the fifth time, the Golden Age of Atlantis emerged. There were High Priests and Priestesses, of which there were twelve at any given time, each in charge of a state, devoted their whole lives to their people. Every decision was taken with integrity and they worked with each other for the highest good for everyone. Of course, they had enormous powers, which included controlling the weather and maintaining the crystal dome (atmosphere) over Atlantis. They frequently poured high frequency healing energy down onto the masses to help maintain the vibration. Consequently there was a Hugh level of love and trust between the people and their rulers. There were volunteers who arrived on Atlantis to take part in this last cosmic experiment, only trees, plants and water awaited them. On previous occasions settlers had been offered a cornucopia of delight and soon fell into greed, sloth, and selfishness. This time, because of the sparse conditions, the newcomers co-operated with each other and pooled their talents for the common benefit. It was this decision to work together for the good of all that created community and enabled them to maintain a fifth dimensional frequency. The first thing they did in each area was to construct a temple where they could meet to give thanks to Divine Source. The people honored nature and had an intuitive understanding of how and when to plant and harvest. Because they were all clairvoyant, they could see the energies of the plants and knew what they needed for their optimum growth. They sang and played music to them, placing appropriately programmed crystals amongst them and as a result harvested plentiful and highly nutritious crops.

NOTES

Because they spent very little time, providing for their basic needs, and without personal ambition, they enjoyed creative and artistic pursuits, loved sports and innocent play and led relaxed, contemplative lives. This developed their right brain capacity and enabled them to attune to all nature including the crystals, the foundation of their incredible spiritual technology. The Atlanteans understood the cosmic properties of water. Every temple had a fountain, villages were surrounded by canals and streams criss-crossed the plains. They built stone circles at points where two streams crossed and angled the stones towards different star systems. They would hold ceremonies and draw in, for example, healing from the Pleiades or wisdom from the Masters of Orion (the Blue Star, Kachina, or the Divine Source's third-eye). This energy would enter their consciousness and that of the water and spread round Atlantis through the system of waterways. So their clear, pure water was constantly filled with high-frequency energy, and when people drank, swam, or bathed in it, they received continuous blessings. We are only now beginning to remember that blessed water carries a special high frequency charge. Throughout the golden ages the people maintained their twelve chakras and twelve strands of DNA, so they literally glowed and radiated. Because they were clairvoyant and could see each other's auras, everyone was honest, so they felt safe. They could transfer pictures from their third-eye to someone else's, so a mother could direct a video of her children playing to a friend in another location. They sent and received clear, direct telepathic messages over long distances. All their words were positive, so not, but, fear or anger was unavailable in their vocabulary. They only had the present tense, so they maintained enlightenment by living totally in the now. All were spiritual healers and could balance each other's charkas but would visit the temple for more advanced healing. Many could teleport, levitate or use telekinesis. If you left something behind you could literally focus on it and draw it into your hands.

NOTES

Soon after a baby was born a priest would examine its aura for the gifts it brought with it. Then the family and community would assist the child to develop and express those natural talents, so he or she grew up with a sense of self worth and satisfaction, doing that which they did well and enjoyed. Small children were encouraged to empathize with and understand animals. Every child had a dog and a rabbit. As he cared for his pets and considered their needs he learned about responsibilities for other creatures. This created a foundation of respect for all things and facilitated a knowing of Oneness. Because everyone was telepathic, a parent automatically knew what their baby needed. However, the little one also belonged to the community which helped to serve his social and educational needs. When they were quite small, they spent part of their day in a nursery, outdoors, where they were cared for and taught to understand the inter-relationship of all things. The temple school was a relaxing place of soft colors and gentle music, where the youngster's spiritual and psychic gifts were encouraged and carefully developed by the priests. They learned self-discipline and elementary mind control. This meant, if a child wanted an orange from a tree, he could focus on the fruit with his mind and draw the fruit to himself. Because they felt safe and secure, they could truly relax the body and mind to receive the cosmic information the priest was imparting to them. They were taught telepathically so that it was easier for them to absorb information. If a student found it difficult to grasp a concept, the teacher would pour pure white light into his or her mind, relaxing every cell even more deeply, after which it could be understood more easily. Special tones were used to assist the children to go into a trance state, during which they practiced visualization, which is one of the first steps toward manifestation. This development of their psychic gifts conferred immense power and responsibility on them and helped them to grow spiritually. The Great Crystal which was pure Source energy was housed in the Temple of Poseidon. It acted as the energy generator and mainframe computer for Atlantis and was linked to a network of crystal pyramids.

NOTES

These were located high above the world and floated in a triangular formation creating a grid of magnetic energy. Each pyramid had a large crystal on top of it and these acted like satellite computers and spiritual sub-stations to the main power station. They were also generators in their own right. The pyramids were antennae that sent signals throughout Atlantis to cells that needed to be charged. This global grid was used to power ability to move through time and space and rematerialize somewhere else. Individuals could even plug into them with their own crystals to draw their personal energy requirements. The people created transports on Atlantis to keep the planet on its orbital path. On the ground, large crystals could draw on it for lighting, heating, transport or any other need. They also acted as batteries in which energy was stored. These generator crystals were used for teleportation that moved in different layers above ground and ranged from airbuses which flew at incomprehensible speeds to individual floating trays which even children could operate. The Magi (priest) could draw materials from other planes and fashion them onto buildings, roads or whatever was required. In this way extraordinary futuristic towns were built with advanced transport and information systems.

NOTES

Where is Atlantis?

The idea that Atlantis would be found somewhere in the mid-Atlantic emerged during the late 19th century. American authors and politicians hypothesize that the lost civilization had been near the Azores. They based their theory on Plato's (the Great philosopher from the era of 347 or 427 BC) description of the continent as lying outside the Pillars of Hercules, which is commonly thought to be near the Straits of Gibraltar. In 1968, pilots flying over North Bimini Island spotted an astonishing geological formation of beach rock that was laid out in straight lines. This area, which came to be known as the Bimini Road, was thought by many Atlantis-explorers to be evidence of the lost continent. In 2004, an American explorer used side-scan sonar to discover an underwater formation 50 miles off the coast of Cyprus. The site sits on top a small mountain nearly a mile below the surface. He believes this site matches point by point with Plato's description of Atlantis. He also believed that the capital of Atlantis once sat on top a mountain, surrounded by shallow lakes in what was once a dry Mediterranean basin. Long ago, the Mediterranean Sea level was lower because it was separated from the Atlantic Ocean by a seawall in the Strait of Gibraltar. Powerful earthquakes breached the seawall, sending a tsunami-like wave streaming across the basin, flattening everything in its path, including Atlantis. Having successfully mapped the site he expects to launch an expedition in a deep-sea submersible to take live pictures and to remove a piece of what he believes is Atlantis. Other explorers of Atlantis have set their sights on the Antarctica. One Argentine explorer states that Antarctica was once closer to the equator. Approximately 10,000 years ago, he insisted, Earth's axis tilted, sending the continent of Atlantis drifting toward its present location at the South Pole. He presents such evidence as the 500-year-old Piri-Reis map (map of Portugal to Brazil), which depicts what he believes to be the coastline of Atlantis.

NOTES

He also points to a 1976 Norwegian expedition to Antarctica, which allegedly found "mysterious structures" that he thinks are remnants of the Atlanteans Empire. Contemporary archeologists suggest that Plato's account of Atlantis's demise is an allegorical retelling of catastrophic natural disasters known in their time. In 1967, off the Island of Santorini, Greek archeologists found the lost city of Akrotiri, buried 4,500 years earlier in volcanic ash. In 2001, archeologists unearthed the ancient city of Helike, which had been destroyed by a massive tsunami spawned by an earthquake, just 20 years before Plato wrote his chronicle of Atlantis. Could either of these sites be the original inspiration for Atlantis? Or were each of these locations as a whole, Atlantis extending all over the Earth, not just in one area.

- *<u>Aryan or Indo-European Root Race</u> characterized by intellect of which humanity is part of today. This race began 60,000 years ago, during the last 10,000 years of the Atlantean Root Race and is still in development. This is also during the time when Shamanism was developed, some 50,000 years ago. A tradition that forms the roots of all healing and spiritual models. A Shaman is a descendent of the Atlantian Root race, a race very spiritually advanced until their destruction. A Shaman is an individual who can through various techniques of drumming, dancing, and dreaming; change their state of consciousness and journey outside time to the realms of magic and mystery. They travel beyond the matrix to contact spirit to seek healing knowledge and power to help individuals and communities. They are spiritual leaders, natural-magic practioner, a priest, a mystic, a counselor, usually in a tribal culture, who is a healer and an interpreter of the unseen world. He or she can divine the future, and walks the path of magic and presides over the rites of passage from birth to death. Their powers are of the five elements (Air, Earth, Fire, Water, and Spirit) which are done during a state of ecstasy or altered frame of awareness. One does not choose to become a Shaman.*

NOTES

The path of a Shaman chooses the individual during events such as near death experiences, high fevers, falling from great heights, life-threatening illnesses, and lucid dreams. Make no mistake to the characteristics of a Shaman and a Madman. A Shaman is someone who experiences a degree of control over his or her otherworld experiences. A Shaman can move between the worlds and can function effectively within mundane and a spiritual context. Not only can a Shaman converse with spirits, but he or she can function concretely and practically within framework of society. A Madman goes off into the otherworld and is never heard from again. A Madman cannot maintain balance, nor can they perceive a difference between physical and spiritual realities. The Madman cannot come back to everyday reality and function effectively within the community. When mad, an individual lacks stability in work, in relationships with other people, and in state of mind. True Shamanism works with their animal totems, for strength in their magical workings as well as their personal protectors. Those who survived are of the more spiritual advanced people of today.

- *Aquarian Root Race which will intertwine with our Root Race of today, it started appearing 50 years ago through the Blur Ray Children, from the Blue Star. Now, imagine a star; a blue star, that moves through the heavens at regular cycle, such as a comet, except this celestial object is pure spiritual energy, a star made manifest by spiritual forces; a star composed of light-beings. These angels- souls- of the highest level-who by their own spiritual evolution, joined together as a singular Host to serve. This Star has moved through the heavens at various cycles, passing slowly at times, pausing other times and appearing to remain still at other times. It has visited the earth many times, most recently 2,000 years ago, when it appeared briefly, moving across great expanses of time in just moments. At that time (it came) to fulfill the prophecies of old and to announce the birth of the Messenger (Jesus) whose task was to remind man of his divine nature.*

NOTES

This same star also visited the earth 12,000 years ago, to warn the world of the coming flood (sinking of Atlantis). 26,000 years ago the Blue Star manifested physical members from its Host to teach the universal Laws of Oneness, or the Law of One. The Blue Star was visible for longer periods at other time frames, such as 54,000 years ago when the turning of the poles occurred. Each time the Star came, it was because it was called and its assistance was needed during the transitions. Once again the Blue Star returns...When the Blue Star makes its appearance in the heavens, the Fifth World will emerge. This will be preceded by the last Great War, a spiritual conflict with material matters. Material matters will be destroyed by spiritual beings who will remain to create one world and one nation, under one power, that of the Divine Source. During this ordeal, this Blue Star will be seen in the heavens for all who have eyes to see. From a scientific point of view it will seem that a new star crossed the heavens and reached the outer fringes of this system in a moment of time. This star, the domain of angelic beings, shall reach out to all who resides on Earth, both physical and non-physical. The hearts and minds of all who are ready to accept their divinity shall transform as if in a flash. At first many will reject this phenomenon, but as the Light bathes all in the realm of existence, more shall awaken. All will see the Light and many will experience higher spiritual vibrations. This shall fulfill the prophecies of old-his Light shall be seen in the clouds. As the Earth comes under the influence of the Blue Star, people will experience many physical changes. The human body will become more sensitive as a result of the new vibrations; the earth's frequency doubles to over fifteen cycles per second. With the new sensitivity, many will "feel" the coming changes. These feelings may be used as an early warning system. Pressures and palpitations in the heart may be felt days or weeks prior to the earth changes. This is a reaction to the shifted electromagnetic fields that are precursors to Earth movements.

NOTES

Electrical sensations in the limbs and spinal column, cramps in the muscular networks, flu-like-systems, migraine headaches, intense dreams-many of which will be actual warnings rather than symbolic in nature-will be a result of the body's sensitivity to the Earth's changes. When one each becomes more" in-tuned" with the Earth, the sensitivity and reaction to the Earth will build. The physical body has already begun change as a result of the new and changing vibrations, and the subtle bodies are almost completely changed. All life, all kingdoms, shall change as a result. A new light-body is being created. As the Blue Star permeates the Earth, greater intuitive abilities emerge, as well as healing abilities. An ability best described as "a knowing" shall be experienced by the many rather than the few. With each passing year, these abilities shall increase tenfold. Inner urges to become more compassionate, more giving, more loving, shall fill all as the Blue Star shines down upon us. When one looks into the sky, two suns shall be present, not one. The new addition will be the small Blue Star, visible in the horizon during the day, and brighter than the brightest evening star or planet. All races of people shall have a bluish tint to the skin as a result. Eyes will become cat-like in order to adjust to the new atmosphere and light, with vision becoming both a physical and non-physical sense. Those who choose shall be able to communicate at will with animals and the other kingdoms, as well as the spirit world. The life span shall be two hundreds years-one hundred fifty years will be like being fifty today. Rejuvenation techniques using Earth's storehouse shall further extend the life span. All the plagues of the nineties shall be gone, including AIDS. Love shall fill the places where before, hate dwelled. Laughter shall be heard in every corner of the world-children responding to love and joy. This is the true "coming", the Great Awakening, the age of the Blue Star. These are indeed blessed times. Could the Blue Star be so important to our times that its presence may affect our development and perhaps even our existence? Only time will tell. All that is needed to move through these times shall be given.

NOTES

What is given are the Blue Ray children who are the forerunners of Crystal and Indigo children of today who are born with a higher knowledge and spiritual development. They are those who come to prepare the way for the next Root Race. Their origin in the inner world has come from those planes of existence that is called the mental levels. It is here that, through their particular sojourning, they have congregated, banned together under the ray that would be blue. Not so much that their skin color would be blue, though this indeed will be a portion of the next root race, but rather their vibratory soul group is of the blue vibration. They have the same soul force vibration as the Atlanteans of Atlantis. Only a few thousand have incarnated and dispersed sporadically around the globe in the mid-1950. The Indigo and Crystal children will come in larger numbers who are the peacekeepers. Only souls who were attuned to the blue vibratory forces while going through the incarnation process (birth) are the true Blue Ray Children. You can identify a Blue Ray child by their aura, blue would be prominent. Also within their eyes, in the iris, you will notice a peculiar wavy action, a shifting or movement, within the color, this is energy, a force that emanates from the structure of the eye. They are drawn to pastel colors, in particular, the color mauve, or hues of mauve. They will also teach their parents, having this ability at birth. All of these gifts are latent in their consciousness, and awaken early. They come to earth consciously aware of most of their own presence in their abilities. They are teaching others at the age of four or five and when these Blue Ones reach the age of twelve they will be equivalent to an adult who has been a teacher for twenty-five years. They are born to parents who are needy that don't have a great nurturing quality because they are to be independent and unattached so they can go into the world and teach. In later times they will evaluate their parent's progress and if none is shown they will force it with a loving hand. They leave home at an early age, and when someone is trying to intimidate them they just smile as if they know this incident will be taken care of by a higher force. They are well protected because they are Light workers.

NOTES

- *<u>The Last Race or the Seventh Root Race</u> will manifest a more abstract level of Beings. These seven races fit into the involution/evolution model, with Atlantis being the middle or the low point. Each Root Race is divided into seven sub-races similar to the Root Race of the same number, the Fourth sub-race being more artistic and emotional, and the Fifth race being more intellectual. The latest sub-race is the Sixth, which only started to appear about a century ago, known as the Indigo Children. This will be the Root Race that the Divine Source will return. This will be the time people come to realize they no longer have control over their lives, and begin to search for the reason Divine Source is disturbing the planet and why the supernatural events are taking place. Many will arrive at the conclusion that humanity has brought this chastisement upon themselves and understand the need for change.*

<u>SNOWMAN SPELL</u>

Make a snowman out of Styrofoam balls, decorate with old buttons, light some red candles, give him a name and chant three times:

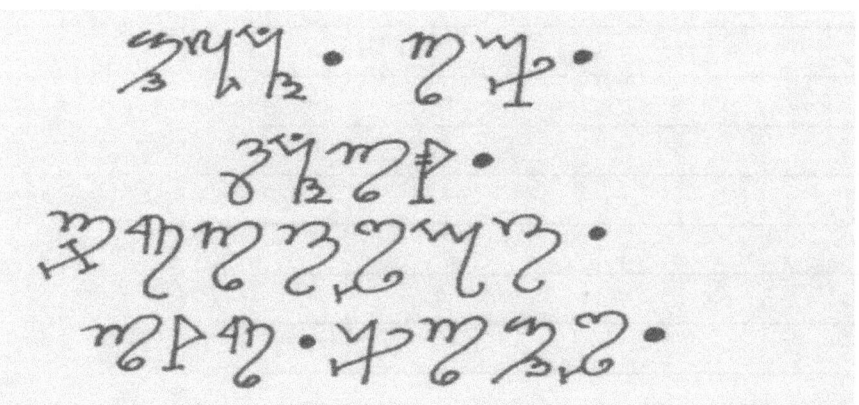

NOTES

DAY 11 / WEDNESDAY/BLUE

Contemplation: 7 X 7 Planes

3. Spiritual Plane:

- *Causal/Spiritual Plane consists of abstract thought from a Higher Human form.*
- *Mental consist of concrete thoughts and is of lower minds.*
- *Astral/Emotional Plane consist of just emotions*
- *Kingdom of Faerie that consist of imagination, rest, recreation.*
- *Lower Astral Plane consists of fear and negative emotions.*
- *Etheric Plane is interfaced with the third and fourth dimensions or the slow to develop spiritually.*
- *Dark Plane consists of Atheist or non-believers.*

BOTTLE SPELL

In a perfume bottle add three drops cinnamon oil, a pinch of nutmeg, a whole clove, pinch of salt, and fill the rest the way with olive oil, use when needed. Light some blue candles and chant with each us

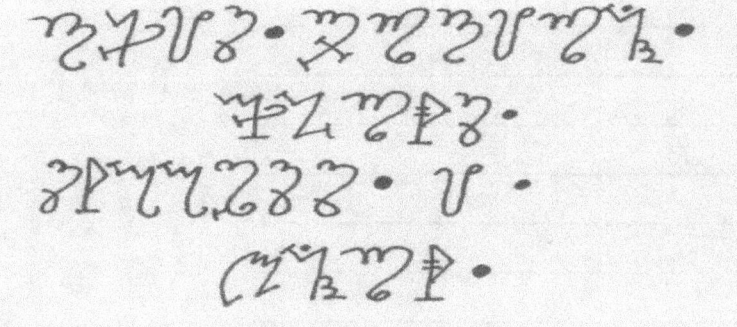

NOTES

DAY 12 / THURSDAY / GREEN

Contemplation: 7 X 7 Planes

4. Intuitional Plane:

- *Atma/Adi, consists of will, breath, soul, and Supreme Being of which are the universal soul and the source of all individual souls.*
- *Buddhi/Anupadaka, consists of Love, Wisdom, one who embodies Divine wisdom and virtue.*
- *Manas I. /Atma, consists of Creative Intelligence and are descendents from the Supreme Being.*
- *Bridge/Buddhi, consists of Harmony and Art, this is considered the bridge between Mankind and the Supreme Being.*
- *ManasII. /Manas, consists of science for evidence of a Supreme Being.*
- *Emotions/Astral, consists of devotion to keep working toward the prior five sub- planes.*
- *Sensations/Physical and Etherical, consists of rituals in service but must not dwell on materialism.*

PROSPERITY SPELL

Watch the sky tonight; visualize the stars throwing good fortune to you. Go inside and light a few green candles, take a shower and again visualize good fortune raining down on you and chant:

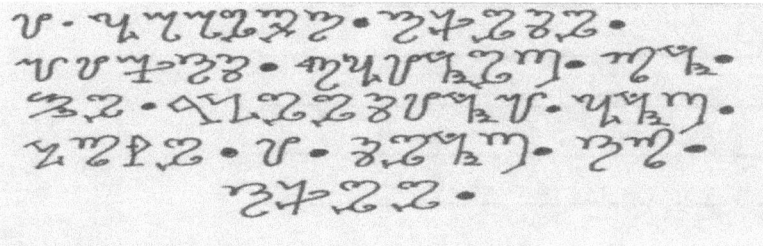

NOTES

DAY13 / FRIDAY / PINK

Contemplation: Friday the 13th.

Friday the 13th became a bad luck day on March 13th 1307. The Templar (Soldiers who protected the Holy Grail, the Holy Grail is actually the daughter's name of Jesus Christ and Mary Magdalene, her name being Sara). On the 13th day on March the armies of France slaughtered nine Templar in order to obtain the Holy Grail, but never found the Holy Grail. They actually thought that Mary Magdalene was the Holy Grail. Looking at the Picture of the Last Supper, look real close to the person on left side of Jesus, it is none other Mary Magdalene. If the French Catholic found the birth document, of Sara, they would have destroyed it. Even today the document is safely hidden until the right moment. Then and only then, will it be revealed to the world. Some say it is buried under a cathedral located in Switzerland. This was such a tragedy when they lost templar knights who were working for spirit. Every year after that on the anniversary of this date they would not do a thing for fear something else would happen tragically. This is where Friday the 13th originated!

NOTES

NEEDED LUCK SPELL

Sit at a table, breathe deeply, meditating on qualities you wish to find in your new lover, light numerous pink candles. Then peel an apple, but do it so very slowly and carefully so it comes off in one long unbroken peel. Stand up and carefully toss peel over your left shoulder behind you so it lands on the floor. The peel will fall into a shape of the first initial of the first or last name of your new love.

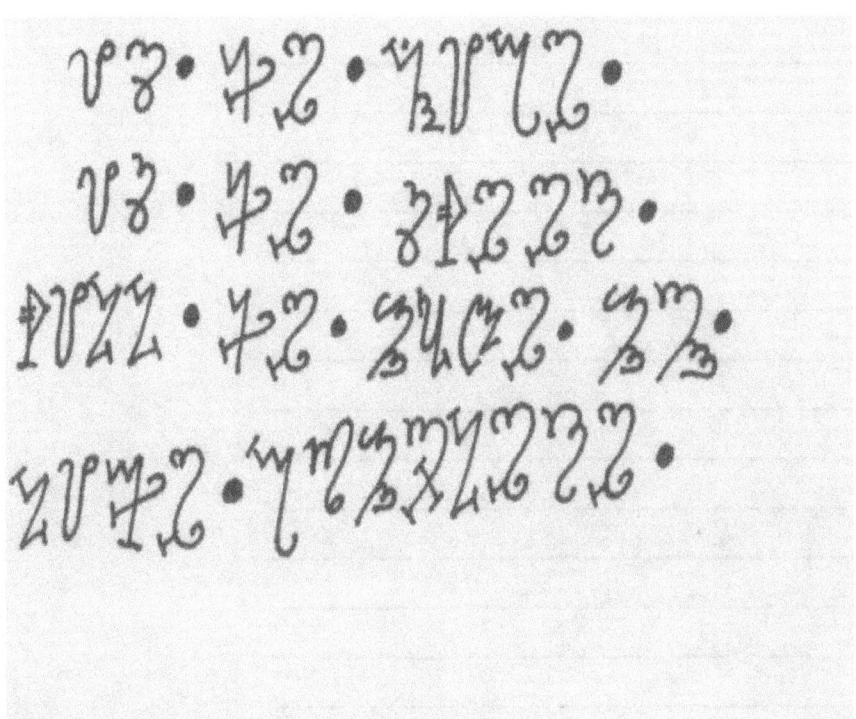

NOTES

DAY 14 / SATURDAY / BROWN

Contemplation: 7 X 7 Planes

5. Mental Plane:

- *Mineral Mind consists of entities that animated the forms of minerals.*
- *Elemental Mind (A) is the realm of the lower elemental forces of nature or are insects.*
- *Plant Mind is the realm of the Plant Kingdom and plant consciousness.*
- *Elemental Mind (B) is a higher elemental force or entity such as gnomes or salamanders that controls the lower level elementals.*
- *Animal Minds consists of the animal level of consciousness.*
- *Elemental Mind © is the realm of more evolved elementals such as Faeries.*
- *Human Mind is the manifestations of life and existence*

RECONNECTION SPELL

Light a brown candle, burn some nag-champa incense, and meditate on reconnecting with your psychic perception or wiring. While in your meditative state, listen to the messages given to you. While writing them in your journal chant:

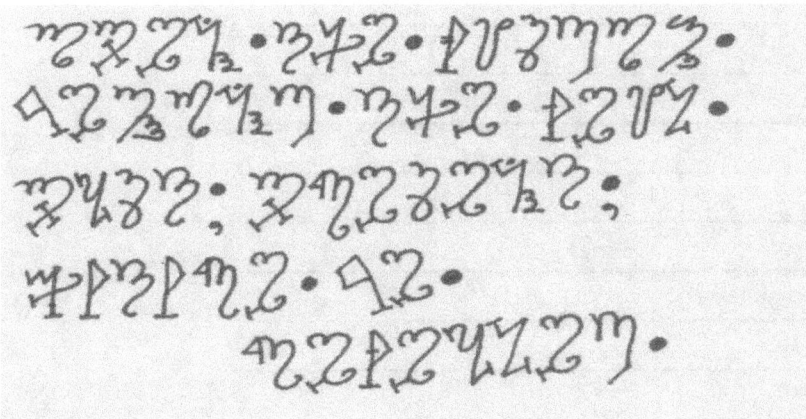

NOTES

DAY 15 / SUNDAY / LAVENDER

Contemplation: 7 X 7 Planes

6. Astral Plane:

- *Mental-Psychic is the higher octave of the physical intellect and the lower of the Divine. It takes on the form of creativity and imagination.*
- *Psychic-Emotional is the octave of higher emotions, especially Love in the highest and purest form and is considered spiritual or heavenly of pure feelings.*
- *Greater Astral is the octave of will, power, and egotism. This is where personalities and individualism comes from.*
- *Lower Astral is a lower level going into materialism or purgatory, where you are faced with Karma debts from your reason, will, and desires.*
- *Astral Light is your antitype double or your dark side*
- *Auric field which is your protection for the physical body.*
- *Chakras are your energy source, but two distinct of the seven are the Manipura A. or the Navel and the Manipura B. which is your spleen chakra, these are where all phenomena imagined by the mind of man have their existence here, as thought-form.*

NOTES

PEACE SPELL

Light a lavender candle, burn some cedar incense for protection, peace, and tranquility and chant three times:

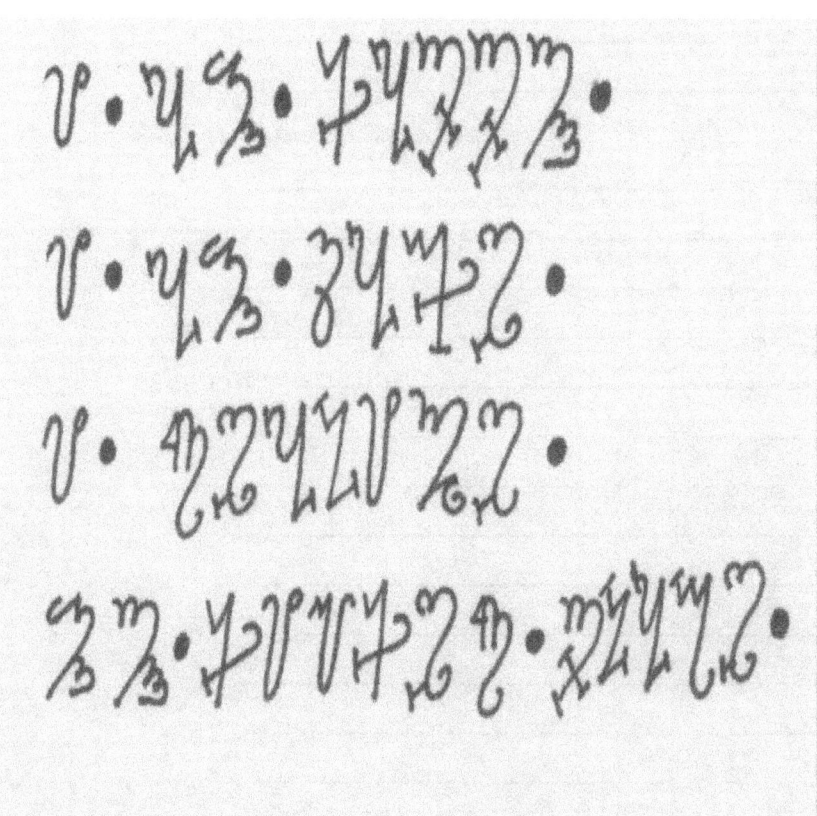

NOTES

DAY 16 / MONDAY / YELLOW

Contemplation: 7 X 7 Planes

7. Physical Plane:

- *Logoic Plane is the Divine Plane of "God" who creates spiritual life from itself and taking the name Logo's (trade mark of all things). Great Beings are on this level.*
- *Monadic Plane is the plane of will where monads, the ultimate divine spiritual sparks in all living things by expressing themselves and evolving and creating on the lower planes.*
- *Atmic Plane is the plane of consciousness and life itself, and where the Great Spiritual Masters are as well as anyone who has achieved the ultimate nirvana.*
- *Buddhic Plane is the plane of true spiritual insight and intuition, this is where the Akashic records are that records and contains history and the sum total of the past of everything everywhere.*
- *Mental Plane is the plane of thought and requires an extreme high state of spiritual evolution. Most Angels and other spiritual beings are found here. Where this plane meets the next higher plane is found what is thought as our souls.*
- *Astral Plane is the first higher non-physical plane. In the out-of-body and near death experiences or right after one dies and before they are reincarnated. The first Guardian Angels are found here.*
- *Physical Plane consists of atoms, sub-atoms, super ethereal, ethereal, Gases, Liquids, and Solids, materialism on the earth plane.*

NOTES

DEDICATION SPELL

Devote your day to doing a tarot reading for someone. Light some yellow candles and your favorite incense and chant before the reading:

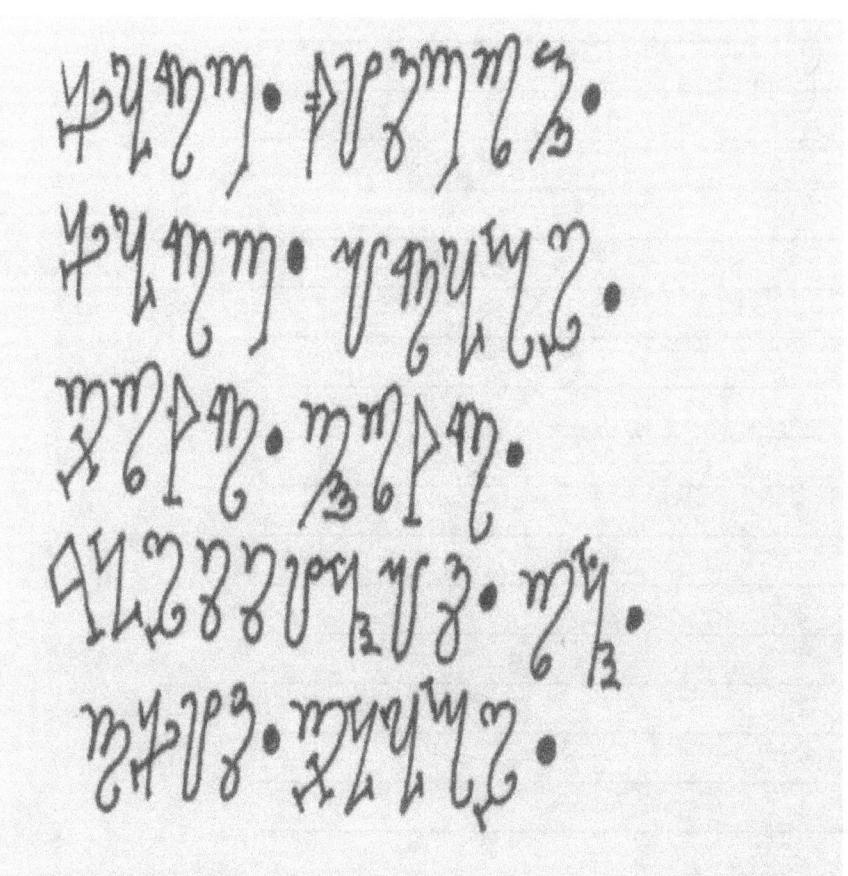

NOTES

DAY 17 / TUESDAY / RED

Contemplation: 4 Earth Vortexes

- *Sedona Arizona, located between Prescott AZ. But closer to Sedona AZ. Near the Mesa Airport. This is one of two positive vortexes; Indians believe these two vortexes are where Great Spirit gives birth to rainbows.*

- *The second positive vortex is in Kauai Hawaii, both Kauai and Sedona are of red rock country. Positively grounding.*

- *The third is the Bermuda Triangle (Devil's Triangle), 1.5 million-square-miles extending from Bermuda to Puerto Rico to the Southern tip of Florida, a place where the laws of physics no longer apply. This is one of two areas on earth where a compass will point to true North rather than magnetic North, the other is the Devil's Sea located in the Pacific around the Miyake Island about 100 km South of Tokyo Japan. This is a negative vortex, which we've all come to know through all the mysteries and fatalities.*

- *The <u>fourth</u> is Stonehenge, in the English County of Sussex, in Salisbury England. It sits on top of the Salisbury Plain and covers 300 square miles and also sit over the largest copper mine in the world, which we all know that copper is a conductor of energy. It is a Sundial, perfectly tracking the Sun in which to form a calendar. This vortex is also considered a negative vortex, maybe because of human sacrifices back in the day of Druids.*

NOTES

ANCESTOR SPELL

Place photos of loved that passed away many years ago, light a red candle and cinnamon incense and work on your mediumship and converse, then chant:

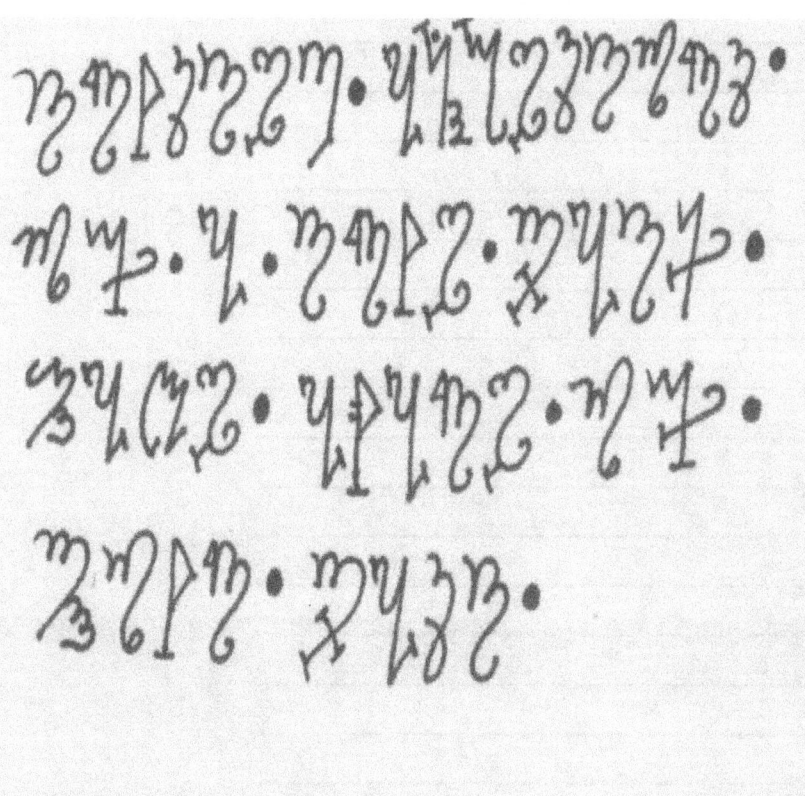

NOTES

DAY 18 / WEDNESDAY / BLUE

Contemplation: Reversed spells are used if you need a spell now, and the Moon is waning, think of the intention in reverse terms. Instead of bringing good health, for example, think of cleansing yourself of the ailment. Instead of drawing for money, think of releasing poverty. Instead of drawing love, think of banishing loneliness. Magic is a craft, a skill, an art, and creativity in your outlook will help you to be more flexible in your work. These are the only spells you should do in a New Moon cycle!

CHILD SPELL

Light blue candles, and your favorite incense, let your child pick it out, and then spend an hour playing their favorite game with them. When the game is finished, have the child nap, play your favorite meditative music, rest, and then chant:

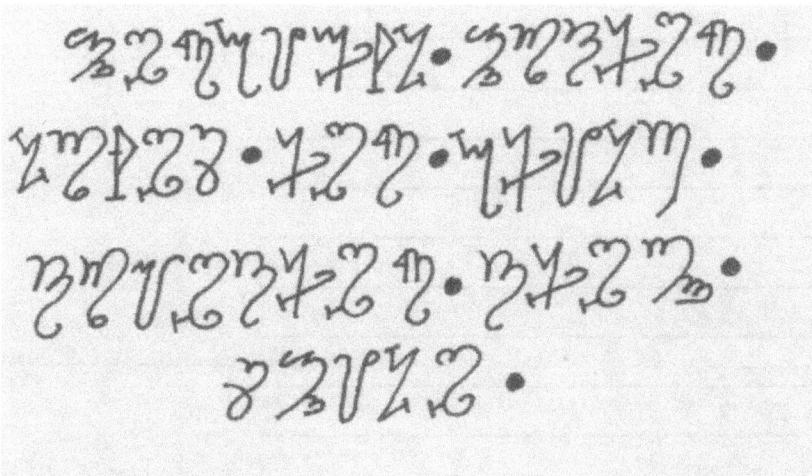

NOTES

DAY 19 / THURSDAY / GREEN

Contemplation: The Goddess Venus

The goddess Venus and the planet Venus are one of the same. The goddess Venus has a place in the nighttime sky and is known as; Venus, the Eastern Star (Ishtar, Astarte). Venus traces a perfect pentacle across the ecliptic sky every eight years. Venus and her pentacle became symbols of protection, perfection, beauty, and the cyclic qualities of sexual love. As a tribute to the magic of Venus, the Greek Gods used her light year cycle to organize their Olympic games.

DIVINATION SPELL

Bring out your cards and do a reading on yourself. Light green candles and some incense, then apply you favorite spread. Before you read chant; try not to manipulate the reading, we have a tendency of doing this when reading ourselves.

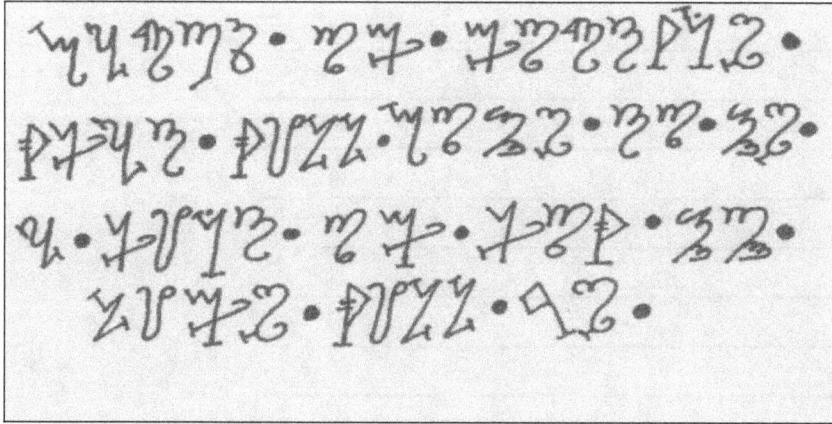

NOTES

DAY 20 / FRIDAY/ PINK

Contemplation: Water scrying done in pools of water provide temporary windows into the fairy realm. Even water captured in a dark bowl or cauldron becomes an open window to heightened perception for those who know how to use it. So it should not be surprising that water divination has had such widespread influence and popularity. Begin by setting a bowl out in the rain, or by digging a small hole in the yard, located near, but not directly under a tree. This is an effective way of creating a window or doorway to the fairy realm. When it fills with water, you have created an intersection between the worlds. Find a comfortable position near the puddle, or if you are using a bowl, place it in front of you. Make sure you will be undisturbed while still being able to look within it. Close your eyes and take a few moments to relax. You may wish to perform a brief meditation and familiarize yourself with nature. With your left hand make several passes over the bowl or puddle, your watery window. This imparts sensitivity to the water and it is also a gesture of an invitation to those spirits or beings associated with it. Be patient and concentrate when gazing into the water. Do not stare intensely. Allow your gaze to be soft and half-focused, as if staring blankly, such as you do when daydreaming. As with crystal gazing, the phenomena will vary. You may see fogginess, like clouds or mist passing by. This is positive, it means that the window is opening, you vision is being awakened. With time, color, images, faces and entire scenarios will appear. Each time you use a rain pool, bowl, or crystal for gazing, your results will increase.

NOTES

LOVE SPELL

Light pink candles, find a photo of your love and one of yourself and lay them side by side on a table. Peel an apple carefully and place upon both photos the peeling from the apple to form a heart and chant:

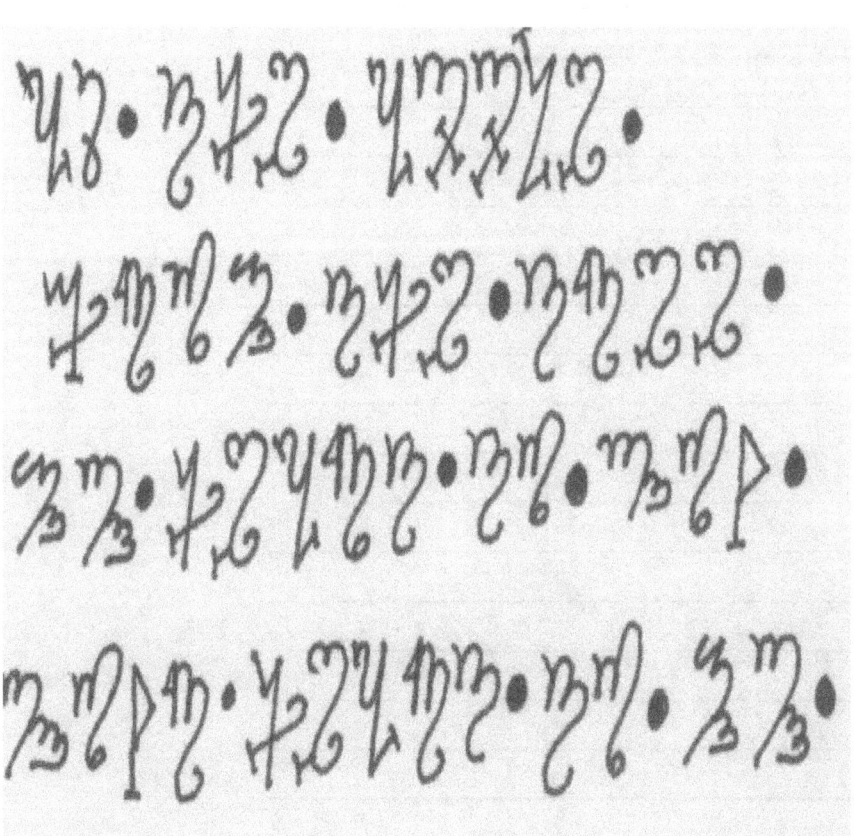

NOTES

DAY 21 / SATURDAY / BROWN

Contemplation: 7 Days of Inspirations

1. Think highly of yourself.
2. No burden is too great for angel wings to lift.
3. Let happiness follow you home everyday.
4. Something you've been working hard for will happen.
5. Hope will not disappoint you.
6. This day will put you one step closer to your dreams.
7. Set a miracle in motion and believe.
8. You can complain because roses have thorns, or you can rejoice because thorns have roses.

PEMDULUM SPELL

Pendulums are not always used for yes and no answers; they also assist in finding lost items. Light a brown candle and your favorite incense. Try to locate something you've been looking for and chant:

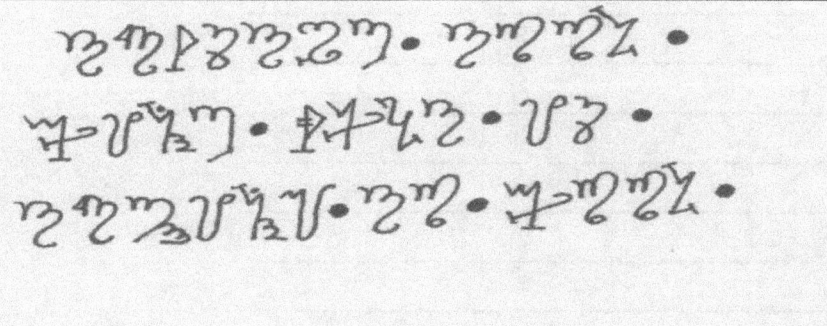

249

NOTES

DAY 22 /SUNDAY / LAVENDER

Contemplation: Opening up to miracles is the key of getting in touch with your inner voice, your intuition. Your inner voice always knows what is best for you and can lead you on the right path to miracles through your spirit guides. Here is how to get in touch with your inner voice. Take a walk with no particular aim or intention. Clear your mind, and just let yourself feel where you body wants to go. You might suddenly find yourself thinking, I should turn right here, or walk to the library. Even if you think your making up the feeling, just follow them. Follow your intuition as your mind relaxes, your intuition will lead you places that are best for you, even if your conscious mind isn't aware of them. You might find a meaningful book, or running into a friend who has an opportunity for you, or just having a sudden brainstorm. The more you practice, the more positive surprises will come your way. Before bed, review your day from beginning to end. You'll discover patterns that will help lead you to more miracles.

SUN SPELL

Light your lavender candle. On some charcoal blocks, light myrrh chunks. Take your hands and raise the heavy smoke up into the sky and chant:

[chant in unknown magical script]

NOTES

DAY 23 / MONDAY / YELLOW

Contemplation: Gift of You! Everyday you give people an amazing gift, YOURSELF! You probably don't realize it, but everywhere you go, your presence is felt and valued for so many reasons. When you ask someone how they are doing, they know you mean it; when you compliment or congratulated them, they know you feel it. When you take time to listen, even when you don't have the time, you show you do worry about them. What's in your heart shows, and it is beautiful.

CHILD'S SPELL

Light a yellow candle and some incense. Have your child or grandchild locate a decorative glass, some sand, a quartz crystal, and five pink stones. Have them put the sand at bottom, stand the crystal in the middle of the sand. Place the five stones around the crystal and have the child visualize it for a few moments and have them chant three times:

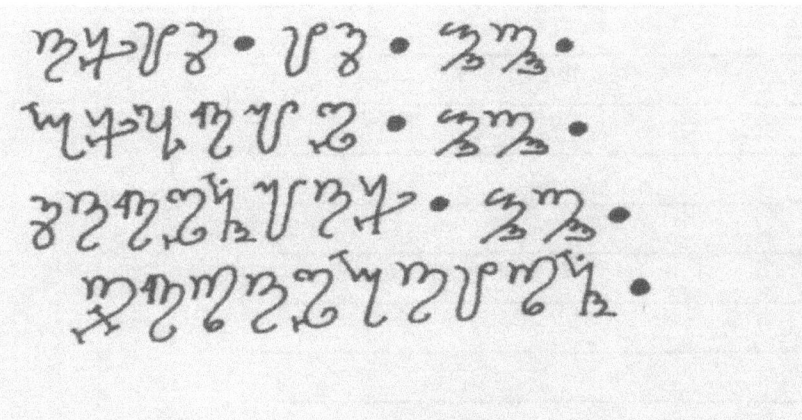

NOTES

DAY 24 / TUESDAY / RED

Contemplation: Connection, How do we get it? Many of us long for deep satisfying connections with people, animals, nature, our deepest selves, and ultimately Spirit. Interestingly, it is through animals first and then nature, that most people have the first connection. For instance, a person's relationship with an animal can provide a clear sense of connection and love...but it's value does not stop there (with that relationship), as it can also be a gateway for them to have similar experiences in other areas of their lives. The core inner story is that the world is filled with caring people, connected to each other and the source. Here I am with my familiars; they are your key to the connection, conversation, and unconditional love. Love you Bruno, Soushie, Loki, my fine fairy friend and Divine Spirit for bringing them in my life.

NOTES

SAFETY SPELL

Light your red candle, light a small fire in a pan, dish, or ashtray, within your kitchen sink for safety. Take some table salt; while sprinkling some into the flame and chant:

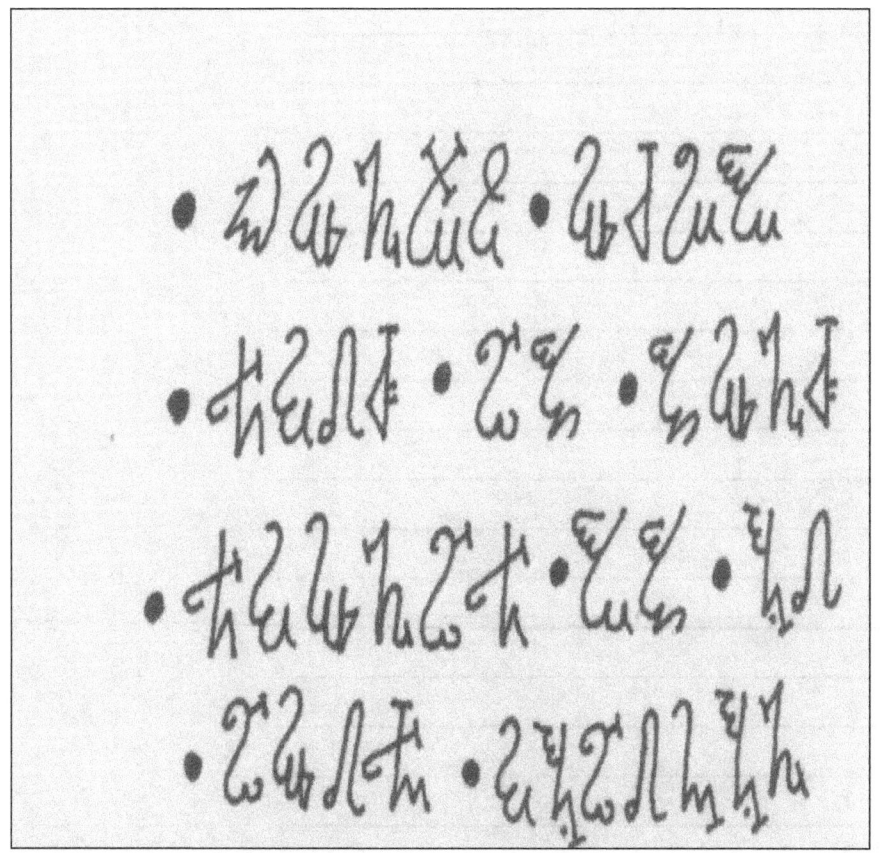

NOTES

DAY 25 / WEDNESDAY / BLUE

Contemplation: We can make a difference we just don't realize how powerful we are. Individually, we have the capability to heal ourselves, transform evil, refurbish mother earth, and establish peace, all with the simple act of intention. Most of us feel impotent in the face of the gigantic political, economics, social, and environmental problems flooding today's world. We consider all the groups we should join to help turn the tides of destruction, but then throw up our hands in futility as we return to our own personal world, already filled with too many responsibilities. We pray that someone else will take care of this huge mess, this undoing of all that we value, our pipeline to the Divine, because we simply can not. We barely manage our own lives, rife with transformational challenges. There is no time, energy, or inspiration remaining to attempt to make the world right. But the Tibetannists' say that we can make a difference. Individually we <u>are</u> the difference. How can we argue our birthright of divine impact as transformational vessels? We're all inherent healers, teachers, and light workers just by the very breath that we share. But we must remember this divine legacy in order to inaugurate the moment-to-moment potency of our effect on the collective consciousness. We've brainwashed ourselves to believe that we are helpless, and ineffective children who make a mess and hope that some adult will clean up after us. Yes, we face colossal dilemmas as we watch our world fall apart. These challenges appear insurmountable from our traditional 3rd dimensional perspective. We must comprehend ourselves as holographic beings. Then we can truly experience the mighty effect that comes from simply the flicker of a new thought pattern, a momentary sweetness that emerges when our hearts soften, or a willingness to suspend our ego's for just a second in order to glimpse at our greater self. We make a difference when we practice our spiritual arts of kindness and reverence for the earth and all living things or beings.

NOTES

Compassion for ourselves and endlessly maintaining awareness that we are part of a bigger picture, acknowledging that our planet is made up of mostly good people and taking a moment to reflect on the presence of our spiritual realm in our lives. So let us dear not succumb to the planetary bad news that increases exponentially that assumes spineless inadequacies that only sustains the brainwashing fostered by the forces of undoing.

<u>**PURIFICATION SPELL**</u>

Light some blue candles, light some incense at your sacred space and chant three times:

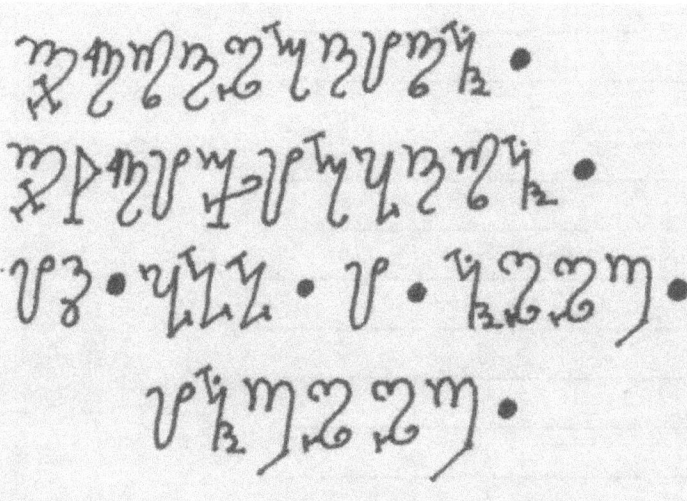

NOTES

DAY 26 / THURSDAY/GREEN

Contemplation: Fairies are of the lower order of spirit beings that exist as the life-force in the natural world, whose task is to maintain. They are ruled by angels. Fairies are closest to angels and resemble them, but with amorphous shapes with white light surrounding them by flowing color auras of energy. Fairies enjoy human company and understand your speech, whatever it may be. They respond well to music and rhymes; they are the ones who send your intentions into the universe. Yes, even fairies have their karmic evolution they must follow to progress to a higher life form. Fairies are divided into groups called companies. Each company comprised of an odd number of individuals ranging from seven to nine members, only one man is allowed within a company. Each company is headed by a woman called the Queen of Fairies. They can either harm or heal; those who honor them with respect will be rewarded with either a grant wish, or a healing. Those who dishonor or insult them is headed by misfortune. If you ever want to encounter fairies, walk by fountains, bridges, wells, towers, woodlands, or beautiful gardens where there is usually a hollow elder tree. This is the doorway to the fairy kingdom. If you breathe in the scent of the elder during mid-summer you will see fairies. They are considered the great spirits of the stars, or nature spirits.

NOTES

SCHOOL SPELL

Light a green candle and some pine incense. Write down something insulting and the person's name that was said to you recently. Roll the piece of paper and tie black thread around seven times then place it in the freezer to freeze their negativity, and then chant.

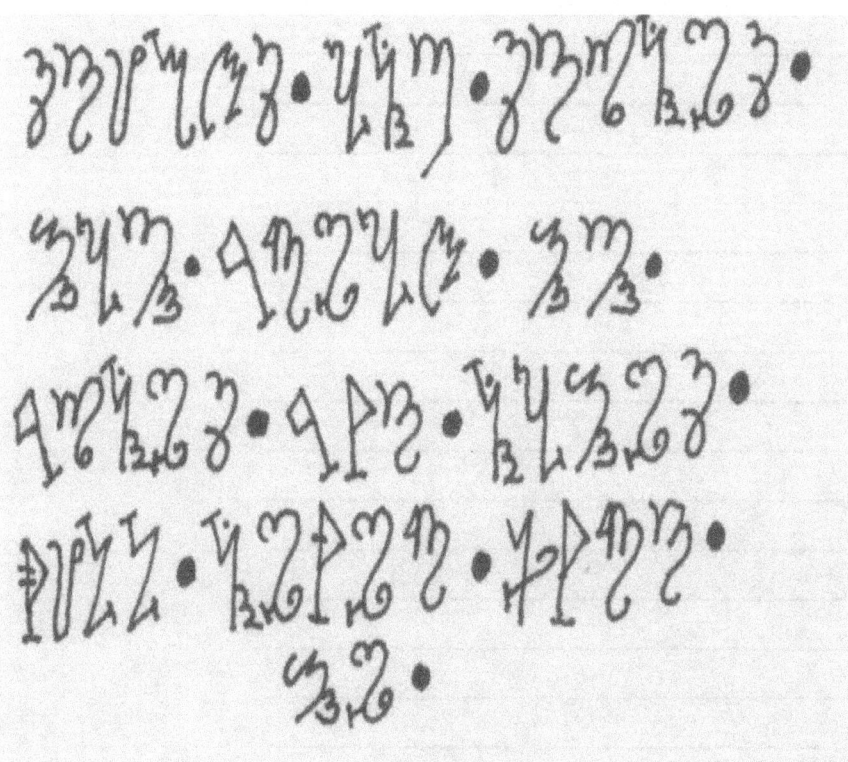

NOTES

DAY 27 / FRIDAY / PINK

Contemplation: The Evil Eye has come under media scrutiny since a little piece of red string, worn to deflect envious and invasive glances, has been seen on the wrists many of today's famous celebrities. These strings come from a skein that was mystically empowered by being wrapped around a tomb in Israel said to belong to the biblical matriarch Rachel. They may be blessed and ties on by rabbis from the Kabbalah Centre, which has branches in many major cities. The strings are worn on the left wrist (the receptive side of the body), and tied with seven knots. Almost anyone who is in the public eye use some sort of protection from the heat of a hostile invisible gaze.

NOTES

LOVE SPELL

Light your pink candles and musk incense. Take a baby book of names, flip through your opposite sex section, close your eyes and stop at a page, before you open your eyes point to a name. This will be your next love, now chant.

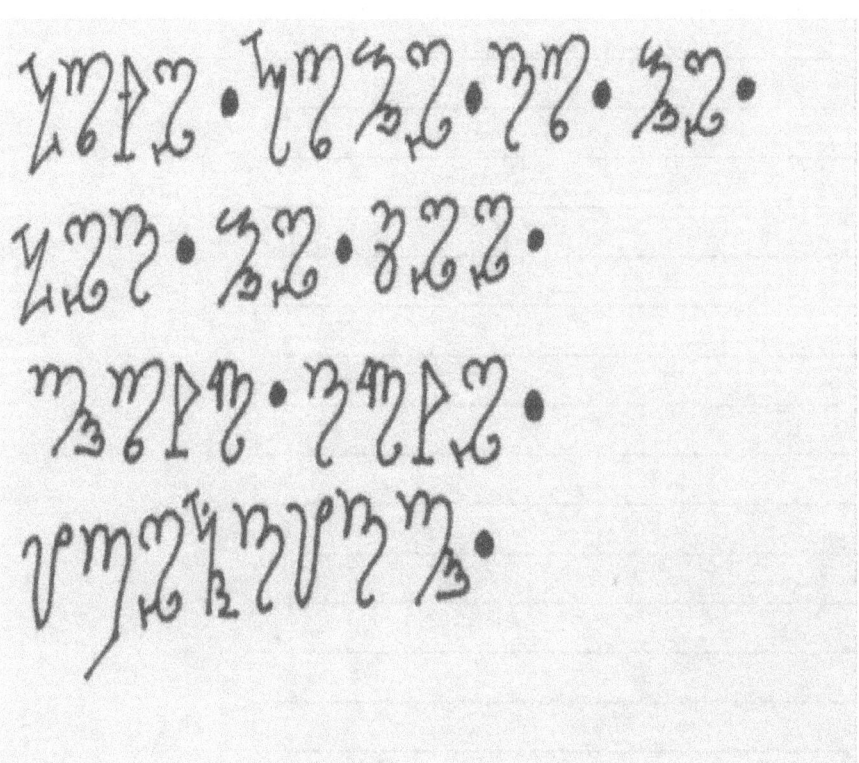

NOTES

DAY 28 / SATURDAY / BROWN

Contemplation: The Power of the Eye and its gaze is a very potent attribute to our animal behavior in the human race. A deep-rooted anxiety about staring goes back to our primal heritage. As animal behaviorists point out, when a large predator fixes its gaze on you, you are in trouble, because that's the animal equivalent of loading a gun and taking aim. The evil eye belief itself is very widespread, but is most prevalent in the Middle East and Mediterranean regions. Opinions vary as to who possesses the evil eye. Some hold the belief that certain individuals have the power to blight whatever they look upon; they may be considered malicious-minded, but sometimes they can be very nice people who don't do it intentionally; it's just an unfortunate power they're born with. Blue-eyed people (not so common in the Middle East) and persons with eye problems or peculiarities are most likely to be suspected. However, others say that anyone of us can convey the evil eye if we look upon something with malice, envy, a little too much admiration, or interest. Babies and bridal couples are especially susceptible to the devouring effect of hungry eyes, and therefore in need of extra protection, though anyone may fall victim at some time or another. The evil eye can also fall upon crops, livestock, and possessions, and may be the blame for things going haywire. If you've been "overlooked", you may experience a sudden-onset headache. Other symptoms can include a stomach ache and/or nausea, diarrhea, fever, a lump in the throat, sleepiness or fitful sleep, lethargy, dizziness, a general feeling of sadness or malaise, and/or a run of bad luck.

NOTES

The symptoms of the evil eye seem to overlap with some other culture-bound syndromes, such as those recognized in the Spanish-speaking world as "espanto" (a type of fright, often brought on by public embarrassment), "susto" (dissociation, often accompanying a fright), and "nervios" (which is a condition of jangled nerves and anxiety). To be cured of the evil eye, people can go to friends, relatives, or local healers, who may give them a ritual washing with salt water or holy water, cense them by burning various herbs and spices, or rub an egg all over their bodies to draw off the bad energy.

RECOVERY SPELL

Light a brown candle, and light some dragon's blood incense. On a piece of paper, write down that you forgive and send healing to this person for what they have done to you and move on, but before you move on, chant this.

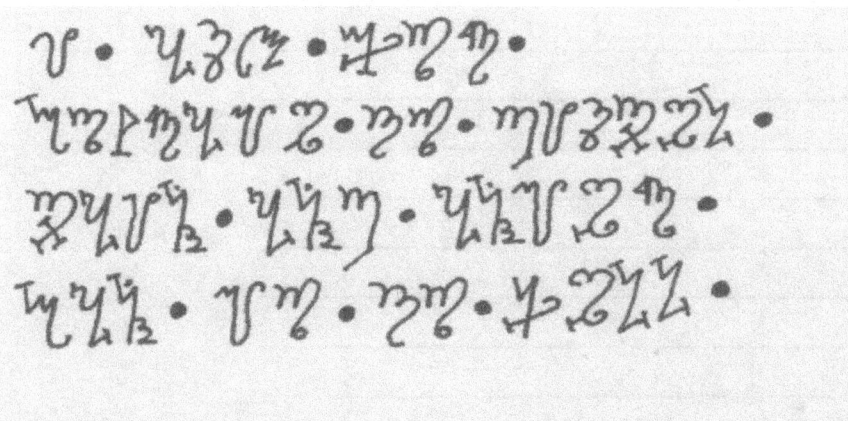

NOTES

DAY 29 / SUNDAY / LAVENDER

Contemplation: Preventing the Evil Eye is primarily accomplished through the use of amulets. In this case of the red string, red is an active color that catches the eye, but also directs aggression back to the sender. For this reason, some older generations of Jews liked to keep something red on hand. Blue-eyed beads are among the most common amulets, perhaps working on the theory that "like repels like" (since, as mentioned above, some cultures consider blue-eyed people to be uncanny). However, blue is also considered protective because it is the color of heaven, and its coolness may counteract the scorching heat that the evil eye is believed to emit. In Italy, you can buy paint in a shade called "defend-against-the-evil-eye blue". Blue is also a favorite color for hamsas-hand-shaped amulets splayed to show five stylized fingers, sometimes with eyes in the middle of the palm. In addition to those eye beads and hamsus that are worn as charms, there are larger versions that are hung in windows or door frames, or mounted on the sides of buildings. Peacock feathers, rocks, and shells with eye-like markings are valued. Jewelry with fantastical figures such as mermaids, the gorgonian (Medusa face), and chimeras (monsters combining the features of different animals) are also considered protective. Bind them in bind them out, and then send them to the Divine Source to heal and deal with them! The general theory is that a person's eye is drawn to shiny or interesting baubles; this deflects the force of the evil eye, because its potency is in the first glance. Gold and silver jewelry and other jewels are also good-again, it's the glint that catches the eye- as are religious icons, and a type of amulet called a corno (a little horn), which is so popular among Italians that the term corno has been generalized to mean and other types of amulets. Spitting three times, certain hand gestures, crotch grabbing, images of male and female genitals, garlic, rue, various plants, and herbs are among the many other things that have been used to ward off the evil eye. All these are fine, but all you really need to do is send the negative energy to the Divine Source, believe me, he'll take care of it for you correctly.

NOTES

BINDING SPELL

Light some lavender candles, and some lavender incense. Take some lavender ribbon and attach something that you constantly loose to your self, purse, or anywhere where it can be found in a moments notice. When you have located this item and tied it chant:

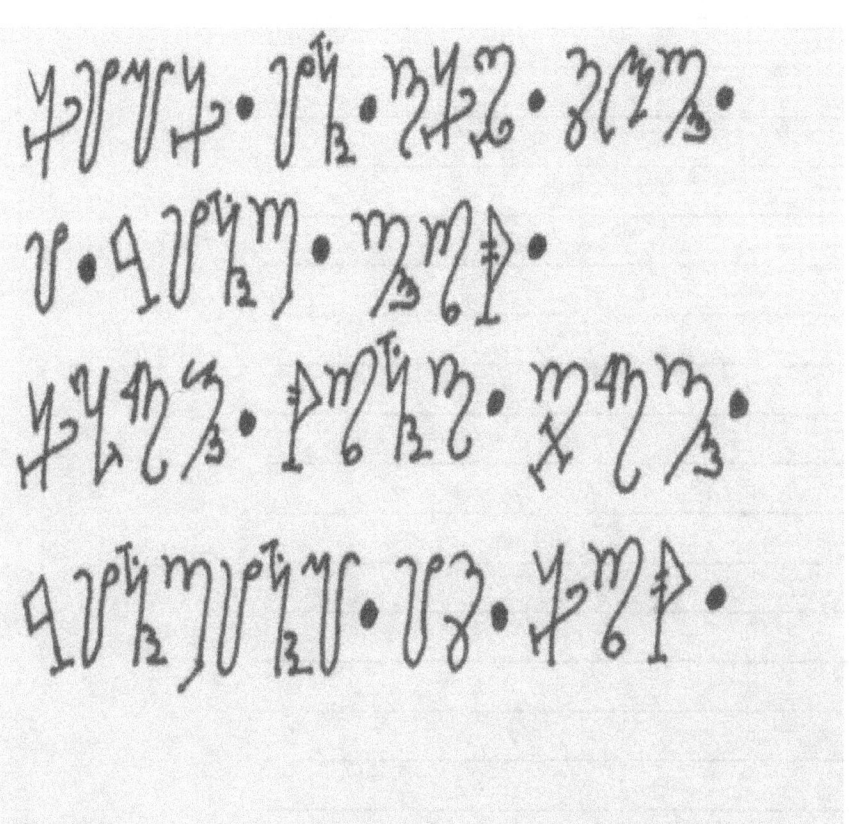

NOTES

DAY 30 / MONDAY / YELLOW

Contemplation: The Evil Eye in the Modern World where anthropologists note that evil eye traditions prevail in societies that have a worldview of "limited good." This is a belief that if one person prospers, others will experience an equivalent amount of misfortune. When there is so much luck to go around, people eye each other with suspicion. Consequently, New Age teachers who spread a philosophy of unlimited good have a potentially spell-breaking effect on society-though they are less likely to be heard in the places where this message may be most needed. Beyond the petty jealousies of some individuals, society itself may exert a sort of evil eye effect, because all societies have systems of surveillance to keep people under control. Social surveillance isn't always intentional and blatant, as it might be under a dictatorship. Even in very permissive societies, surveillance evolves organically and operates through institutions like religion, education, laws, government, and customs-and also through popular culture and the natural tendencies of humans to observe and talk about each other. Consider, for example, how young people feel pressured if their clothes or mannerisms are out of step with their peers. They may not be attacked or criticized by any specific individual (though some will), but all will experience the gaze of disapproval. Surveillance affects us at all stages of life; even in private, we have a certain sense of being watched. Surveillance isn't always a bad thing, because it compels people to treat each other decently. Nevertheless, it registers on a subliminal (buried deep within your subconscious mind reappearing when least expecting, causing havoc with your association with others) level. It may contribute to free-floating anxiety in sensitive people and trigger paranoia in schizophrenics, but all of us feel it. If we are aware of this surveillance, we can use some evil-eye counter-magic techniques as a way of reasserting our individuality.

NOTES

Thus, wearing a red string, a corno, or an eye bead can be the way of telling society, "I'm aware of your surveillance," and "right back atcha!" You can either tell them you outgrew the baby monitor, or would you me to purchase you either a set of binoculars, or cam-corder for the next occasion? Then smile gently and walk away calmly. Because of your smile and calmness, you will surprise and confuse them which blocks their negative energy they're trying to send, but, unable to send because of the block you just put up.

SLEEP SPELL

Light your yellow candles and some sandalwood incense. Ring a bell nine times, put some rosemary herb in a small muslin bag and tie tightly and place under your pillow and chant:

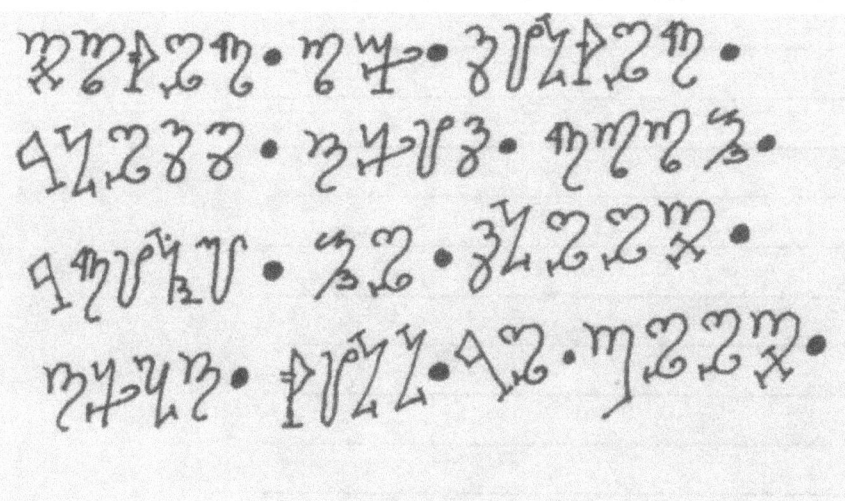

NOTES

DAY 31 / TUESDAY / RED

Contemplation: Although the public gaze can have an evil-eye effect, people of goodwill can transform it into a gaze of blessing and use it as counter-magic against the spell-binding influences of certain disturbing types of social transactions. A typical example is when you witness someone being rude to a waitress, cashier, or other service person. The target of this hostility may go home feeling upset, quite likely experiencing some of the symptoms traditionally ascribes to the evil eye or espanto. However, because verbal abuse (and other displays of aggression) will also subliminally affect by standers, those who witness it may also develop many symptoms of unease. This is a condition of a variety of "common shock." In an uncivil society, the effect of common shock is cumulative-likewise for people who live in even mildly abusive families, and for others who regularly witness what goes on in such families. I recommend "compassionate witnessing" as an antidote to common shock. When you are in the presence of verbal violence or other hostile interactions, you can reassure the victim by saying something like "I'm sorry that person was so rude. I hope the rest of your day will go better." In so doing, you are acknowledging, "I saw that," but let the other person know, it's OK, I'm not judging you-I know it's not your fault." Calming words combined with a friendly look while witnessing the evil eye at work immediately counteracts. Of course, to cultivate the eye of blessing, you must consistently purge yourself of negativity, and look upon the world with kindness and openness. If you are wearing an evil ye charm, let it carry this additional meaning for you! Smile with kindness and openness, it confuses your opponent to where they're incapable of sending bad energy.

NOTES

WAND SPELL

Go outside and find a small old branch that fell from a tree. Take it home and if there is bark on it, strip it clean. Light some red candles and musk incense. All you will need to do to your wand is polish it daily, by doing this you charge it with your own energy. When you are finished cleaning and polishing it chant:

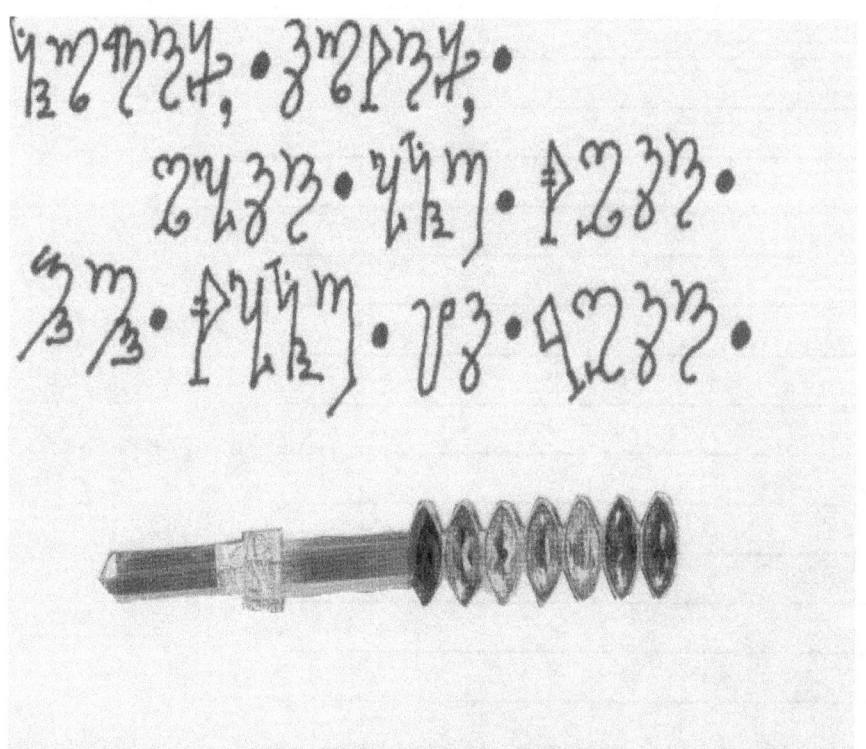

NOTES

CHANT TRANSLATIONS

- *Hail divine, keeper of keys, turn protection over to me.*
- *Future calls, turn the wheel, my dreams revealed.*
- *Bar this door with discipline, let no evil in.*
- *Is it yes, is it no, please tell me so.*
- *Hear my chatter, money is the matter.*
- *Like a circle, we are bound, from this bean, our live is sound.*
- *By knot seven, all desires are in heaven.*
- *Voices of spirit speak to me, give wisdom and harmony.*
- *Bless this home for joy to come.*
- *Man of snow, protect our home.*
- *This potion flows, success I know.*
- *I accept these gifts rained on me, blessing and love I send to thee.*
- *Is he nice, is he sweet, will he make my life complete.*
- *Open to wisdom beyond the veil, past, present, future, be revealed.*
- *I am happy, I am safe, I realize my higher place.*
- *Hard wisdom, hard grace, pour your blessings on this place.*

NOTES

CHANT TRANSLATIONS
Continued

- Trusted ancestors of a true path, make me aware of your past.
- Merciful mother loves her child, together they smile.
- Cards of fortune, what will come to me, a hint of how my life will be.
- As the apple from the tree, my heart to you, your heart to me.
- Trusted tool, find what is trying to fool.
- I give honor and praise, thanks for sunny days.
- This is my charge, my strength, and protection.
- Ancient fire in my hearth, warm me forever, with your spark.
- Protection, purification is what I need indeed.
- Sticks and stones may break my bones, but names will never hurt me.
- Love come to me; let me see your true identity.
- I ask for courage to dispel, pain and anger can go to hell.
- High in the sky, I bind you now, harm won't pry, binding is how.
- Power of silver, bless this room, and bring me sleep that will be deep.
- North, South, East, and West, My wand is best.

NOTES

CHAPTER VII

SPIRITUALISM

This is where my transition with Wicca mixed with Spiritualism begins. They do not believe in death, they believe in continuity and their Declaration of Principal are their ten commandments which all speak of the continuity of life and that we make our own happiness or unhappiness. There is only one thing that troubles me within this religion, and that is within their classes they continue to teach from the dark ages, back in the days of the Fox sisters (Catherine, Leah, and Margaret,) who brought about spiritualism through rapping and tapping of their spirited friend, this too place in the year of 1848, in Hydes, New York, where shortly after, on March 31 of that year spiritualism was born. Maybe this is actually why I find peace and love within this tiny church. I have never found as much acceptance in one place before; they're of the same minds. This is one church I do enjoy and is allowed to be who I am, a psychic medium and am accepted for it. I sincerely thank the First Spiritualist Church of Salem, Massachusetts for the feeling of total peace within, my spiritual growth and membership into their family. We are born with psychic abilities and it should be recognized within everyone. It doesn't matter if you're a Spiritualist with the Declaration of Principals, Wicca with the Wiccan Rede, Christian and their Ten Commandments, or any other religion, all religions lead to the same thing, "the Divine Source."

NOTES

Spiritualism believes in all natural laws; too numerous to mention; all are incorporated within their Declaration of Principals:

- *We affirm in Infinite Intelligent.*
- *We believe in the phenomena of nature both physical and spiritual are expressions of Infinite Intelligence.*
- *We affirm that correct understanding and living in accordance, constitutes true religion.*
- *We affirm that the existence with personal identity continue after a change of death.*
- *We affirm that we do communicate with the so-called-death which is scientifically proven over and over time after time.*
- *The Golden Rule contains the highest morality which is "Treat other like you want to be treated."*
- *We affirm that we make our own happiness or unhappiness by obeying or disobeying all natural laws, this is your own moral responsibility.*
- *We affirm the doorway to reformation is open to all souls here and hereafter, but refuse to be influenced by any spirit below you in mind or in character.*
- *We affirm precepts of Prophecy and Healing are the highest attributes proven through mediumship.*

NOTES

NOTES

INTRODUCTION TO MEDIUMSHIP

Any advice that can be given to allow students to demonstrate mediumship is to show the manner true medium thereby becomes a participant in the divine plan to the further of good. Mediumship is superior to race, religion or color, and there is no reason why any medium cannot continue to observe any religious observance he or she chooses, and to incorporate the mediumship within it. In the past mediumship has existed in many phases; it to, has progressed, which you can develop these gifts of spirit and should be accurate and simply expressed. It is not necessary for a person to be a man or woman of letters or to be educated in psychic science to become a medium. In the past there have been many instances of simple folk being outstanding mediums. Many people wish to become mediums, to see the spirit people, hear them speak, obtain counsel, heal the sick, help the bereaved, give advice and assist those who are in need. This desire is sometimes simply that of satisfying your personal ego, to be different from other people, the wish to be recognized, and to be placed on the mantle of mysticism. This is an entirely wrong approach to mediumship. Mediumship has a purpose, and that is to demonstrate to man that he is not just a physical being, but that he is a part spirit, that this life is but an apprenticeship for the greater and fuller life that commences with the physical death. That through this knowledge mankind will receive the drive to adopt an enlightened code of values that in its evolvement will outlaw war, poverty and the other immoral trends in our present way of life. The true motive that inspires mediumship is a spiritual one. If this is not so, then self discipline (the latter quality is most essential). There is no reason found for the great efforts of the evolved personalities in spirit life, the teachers, philosophers, doctors and others, to use human instruments for the progression of all souls. Therefore, a student to mediumship should possess that inner yearning to be used for the higher purpose, and to view their education of mediumship as a means to help others.

NOTES

It should be the denial of selfishness and the giving of the self to a spiritual purpose, knowledge and understanding of the spiritual directive. It has survived attack, ridicule and opposition, until today it is respectable and acknowledged by scientists, religious leaders, the press, an Archbishops' Commission, and the law of England. All forms of mediumship is an exact spirit science, but cannot be assessed by analysis or material values; it cannot be put under the microscope. Through our inability to fully comprehend the science of mediumship, an air of mysticism has surrounded it, and this has, at times, given rise to questionable practices and opinions. Today, there are a great number of development classes being held in the Spiritualist Churches and in home circles. Mediums who conduct these are sincere, good people, and are understandable that owing to a lack of true appreciation of what mediumship actually is, all sorts of traditional practices have arisen. These practices have been handed down from medium to medium through repetition, and have become accepted as being true, when in fact, they may not be. Later on these practices will be referred to and reasons given why they should not be adopted any more. You should not attempt development if you are neurotic or fearful. Mediumship needs a mind that is strong, purposeful and capable of self discipline. A physical deformity or affliction need not to interfere with your development of mediumship, but it is again stressed that any student to mediumship should be of sound mind and capable of forming balanced judgments and to impose accurate information. It is awesome to give a reading and know you've hit onto something or connected. I recently did a reading for a client and her mother came through. I described her thoroughly. One thing puzzled me though; she came through with a toy fire truck. So I said to the client, does a toy fire truck mean anything to you? She broke down in tears and said that her mom used to scold her for playing with it instead of dolls, and hid it in the attic.

NOTES

She continued to say that just the other day, she was going through her mother things in the attic, and came across the toy fire truck and placed it on the mantel in her living room. Needless to say her mom was chuckling and soon the client was also. You must give all information offered even if it doesn't make sense to you; it may to your client. During our mediumship class, I went to another student and brought through her father, described him in full attire, the very next week, this student brought in a picture of her deceased dad, it was amazing of how accurate mediumship is. These are only a few experiences; they are my best for evidence. Remember full descriptions of the person, their surroundings and anything odd to you, bring it through, it's not silly, it's what you see.

NOTES

EYE OF YOUR MIND

At this early stage it is essential for a student to understand the way in which your consciousness operates. This simply can be explained by regarding your consciousness as an eye (Third-Eye). Onto your Third-Eye, is projected all physical thought, sensation, pain, and your experiences arising from your senses. In life, the Third-Eye is never free from any impressions, thought pictures, recollection from memory, etc., in one form or another. When you "see" or "hear," it is not your eyes or the ears that see and hear. Your organs receive vibrations or impulses, and these are transmitted along your nervous system to your brain, where they are translated into recognizable experiences that are projected onto the Third-Eye of consciousness. In hearing, sound impulses are converted into an intelligent appreciation of their meaning by virtue of your knowledge how to interpret the result into words, with meanings we understand. The use of the term "Third-Eye" will be constantly referred to throughout this chapter, and therefore it is important that you should clearly understand how this works. You possess in addition to physical perception through the ordinary mind a spirit mind. This is concerned with your reception of impressions, experiences and thought pictures from a spirit source. The Third-Eye is able to receive these spirit experiences when your eye is unoccupied by physical ones. Your consciousness is unable to hold two distinct sets of thought impressions at the same time. The developing medium is in need to learn how to clear the Third-Eye of physical thoughts allowing it to receive spirit thoughts and impressions. Thoughts of objects are presented into the Third-Eye as pictures. For example, if you close your eyes and think of a common object, such as a pencil, a presentation of this will be projected into your Third-Eye in the form of a picture taking on the characteristics of which you conceive it to be. If your thought of a pencil is qualified by the suggestion of an "ever sharp" pencil, the picture will alter from a common wooden one into a silver automatic pencil in that sort of picture in your Third-Eye.

NOTES

If a spirit guide wishes to convey the thought of a pencil, your Third-Eye would receive a picture in accordance with the characteristics of the pencil presented to it. Another example might be that your guide conveys the thought of "mother." Your Third-Eye would then receive a representation of your mother as would naturally come from the general recollection of your mother as remembered or as described. This aspect will be dealt with in detail when we come to consider clairvoyance. The present purpose is to give a simple over-all explanation of the method by which we "see" and "hear" from the spirit communicator. Observe that your physical mind works in the closest harmony with the spirit mind and both have the common meeting place in the Third-Eye of consciousness. The same process applies with inspirational, or trance, and speaking. In this, your guide will transmit a flow of thought sequences through your spirit mind into your Third-Eye of your consciousness where it will be converted into the form of words to clothe your thoughts according to a medium's knowledge of language. If you possess an extensive vocabulary the thoughts from spirit will be better expressed than with one whose knowledge of words is more limited. The better a medium is mentally equipped; the better the presentations of mediumship.

NOTES

IMPORTANCE OF SILENCE

When you walk into a typical developing circle, you are sitting under the leadership of an experienced medium. You are told to "enter the silence," to "concentrate." To do this, focus your thoughts on a cross, a flower, or to imagine you are looking through a long tunnel, with emphasis on your need for prolonged concentration. I was informed that if I did this my mind would become blank and my guides would take control. This process, with variations, is the customary routine in many development circles for students. In light of experience, I now see how more thorough this initial training could be. By concentrating in any direction the Third-Eye was strongly occupied by my own thoughts, obstructing any contact of spirit communication. The word "concentration" is commonly used during development. It is an incorrect word, giving an incorrect idea. A superior directive would be allowing "abandonment" of thought to take place. True contemplation of a beautiful symbol helps in meditation, which, not actual development is helpful in the success of mental relaxation as a introduction coming from abandonment of active physical consciousness, is to leave the Third-Eye open, and to assist in the appearance of your guides. How do you make your mind blank? Is there any set line of advice that can be given to show how it can be specifically attained, it is such a personal matter, needing individual adjustment to suit varying temperaments and personalities. It is a delicate condition that arises from the ability to meditate with relaxation. In the section "Early Development," I will give some instructions how this can be attained. When there are arguments present try to avoid involvement, you are only inducing yourself with their negativity, so if it's not your fight stay out of it. If you're in a situation that you feel needs correction and it has nothing pertaining to you, stay out of it. You have a lot of work that needs to be done and you must not weigh yourself down with other people's problems. This person or people may have to fight their own fight to correct their own path.

NOTES

By getting involved, may take you off your correct path as well. My suggestion is walk away, or if your opinion is requested, stay neutral; this will set a great example for others. Remember you do make your own happiness and unhappiness, so walk away from any negativity. Others will follow your example, if not; spirit has a way of working things out to be correct. This is your first step for a quiet mind; their negativity is no longer your negativity. There is a certain magic that happens when we listen to ourselves or to what another is saying or not saying. Silence allows the penny to drop and the impact to be felt. In fact, silence speaks volumes if we just take a moment to listen! It is certainly an art to know when to speak and when to let silence prevail. There is the saying it is better to remain silent than to be thought a fool. However, silence is more than a cover to hide behind. Silence is indeed a language, a pathway that a spiritual mind must walk along to truly discover the self. Our ability to communicate is crucial for our survival and development. In some parts of the world people learn to speak several languages out of the need to survive. Our ability to speak is a wonderful expression of our freedom and letting those around us know how much we care or that we are OK. For novices entering "the silent path," the quiet can indeed feel uncomfortable, but this phase will pass, as one realizes just how rewarding this space can be. There is no need to fill those "empty" moments with chatter of one kind or another. Just remember: we are born out of silence and will return to silence again. Silence is more than the absence of words. For a yogi, silence begins in the mind. Words are weighed carefully, for they are energy and we are often drawn to such souls as they touch our core. Silence of the mind signals a soul walking the path of peace and one who has experienced the wisdom found in stillness. For these souls, silence is indeed golden. I am a peaceful soul! See how nature-trees, flowers, grass-grows in silence; see the stars, the moon and the sun, how they move in silence...we need silence to be able to touch souls.

NOTES

Silence is a Virtue For a Blank Mind

NOTES

NEVER A BLANK MIND

Many students are told to look for their minds becoming "blank" (condition of unconsciousness) the majority of students expect this state of consciousness to come, some refuse to let themselves go further until blankness robs them of consciousness. So let this be plain and simple. It is quite impossible for your mind to become "blank". No one can consciously or purposely induce this state. So long as you are conscious so must the Eye of the mind be occupied in some way. Even when we sleep the mind is not 100 percent incoherent, it is aware of sound and your physical being. Your Third-Eye is never blank, even under anesthetic; the mind is coherent and working. Dreams are a result of mental activity. In dreams, projections into your Third-Eye, thought pictures, sometimes in a disordered way, your thoughts run free without any directive control by the self. It is when these thought impressions are strong that your consciousness recalls them when you wake. Some mediums say, for the purpose of romanticizing their gift, to seek prestige or to impress others, which their minds become quite blank when in trance or under control of their guides, they also say they "do not remember anything that has taken place. Like I said previously, it is impossible for you to become completely blank, the object is to control what flows in and out. The way in which a student obtains contact with their guides is by the means of attunement. This has already been referred to prior, but needs further comment. This should be the first step for the beginner to seek a way of attunement. This can be simpler than may at first appear possible, for this is really all development consists of- plus experience. The ease of which attunement develops is dependent upon the degree of affinity established through sitting through development. To experienced mediums, attunement will become second nature; if they are clairvoyant they must always first establish attunement to clear their Third-Eye to receive spirit vision, and usually they are able to attain this condition in but a second or so.

NOTES

A student should seek this condition of receptiveness by abandoning conscious thought directives and surrendering their physical mind to allow their inner, or spirit-self, to become their higher-self. It is this condition that establishes the flow of thought, either in picture or in words in thought form from a spirit source which can be received in the Third-Eye for the medium's consciousness to perceive. In the olden days, a student needed to learn how to hold spirit impressions and to continue to follow on without imposing any interference from their questioning mind, as it is so very hard to do, thus breaking off your attunement. This oneness and affinity with your spirit guides can be sustained as a student becomes used to "listening to one's-self, and so allow the communication to flow on, unrestricted. This involves a delicate state of mental adjustment, and there is hardly any dividing line between a spirit communication and one's conscious thought. Thoughts can so easily intermingle. A student needs to encourage their mediumship and so it is best to accept all such impressions as coming from spirit but with an inner reserve as to whether the incoming thought flow is from a literal spirit source. They should not be rejected, but accepted, assuming the probability that they emanate from a spirit source. In the same way, and for the same reason, it is unwise to accept every statement purporting to come from a guide, even in a trance state, as literal spirit. It has repeatedly been noted in the rear cases when a medium is in a total trance state and that they are truly unaware of anything that is being said nor done, their sub-conscious knowledge or desires can influence the words that are spoken. It is always best to accept any utterance made under spirit influence with reserve and await confirmation in some other way. It is wise to subject any advice that is given to study and judgment by common-sense. When a student is told that their guides are so-and-so, he should accept this with reserve and await confirmation from another medium that is unaware of the previous pronouncement.

NOTES

With the experience and usage the medium by their guides, the developing medium will soon be able to ascertain from their inner knowledge of "knowing" whether the intuitive impression or experiences they receive are under control or are inspired from those on the other side of life. All equal rights; feminism; ecology; attunement; brotherly/sisterly love; and planetary care are all part in the acknowledgement of a holistic universe and a means toward the rising of higher consciousness.

SPIRIT GUIDE

We live and grow in a world where there is virtually no veil between our world and the world from the other side of life. It is natural to me to connect with the spirit world of guides at all times. I not only asked my spirit guides for assistance, I feel their presence and received help 24/7. With their help my life is magical, fulfilling, positive and always protected. To me it was natural and I assumed everyone had the same experience. As I grew a little older I sadly realized that this loving world of spirit is not known to too many people. It may be because of industrialization and intellectualism that has snatched them from our hearts and from the place we meet and commune with spirit; and planted us totally and physical in our heads; the place where egos reign over us with threats of seclusion and extinction. When we live in our physical heads we not only missing out on our own spirit and our own natural connection with the spirit world, we miss the magic they bring us as well. With a little effort you can reconnect with your guides because as spirit yourself it is only natural for you to connect with the spirit world. It helps if you understand exactly who your guides are and where they come from. I have several Spirit Guides, one is a Tibetan Monk, and his real name is Tuttle but wishes to be called turtle. I believe him to be a Master Teacher. My Second is a Muse; her name is Flora, she is lovely, creative, a great sense of humor, and speaks truthfully and bluntly.

NOTES

Another looks of Asian decent; when he first came through he stated his name is unimportant, after working with him for over nine months, he finally revealed his name as Ingram which is not at all Asian. He works very quickly with high intensity, I believe him to be an Ascended Master, because he is of a higher vibration with enormous knowledge, which he shares with me gratefully. I'm sure there are a few more that pop in and out from time to time to learn from me or my spirit guides. Like people, there are many levels of spirit guides and non-physical entities and energies in the spirit world. They all vibrate on their own unique frequencies, simultaneously sending unique signals. Each guide has its own frequency, some higher than others, like specialists waiting to help us on every issue in our world. Some guides are past family members, loved ones, some guides are from past lives that you've shared; and most guides come in as spiritual teachers to help direct your path. Guides make your practical day to day routine run smoother. Nature spirits and elementals connect you with the earth; animal spirits are to guide you on any journeys you undertake and to teach you unconditional love, responsibility, and nurturing. Joy guides are usually small children who keep your spirits high and make you laugh when life becomes overwhelming and painful. There are also angels, saints, divas, masters, and of course the Alpha and Omega of all guides, living and loving very close to the Divine Source. The spirit world is as populated as ours; different guides working on different frequencies all the time to help you. This shows how wonderful, loving, and generous our Divine Source is toward us. No matter what we face, or what we desire, we have a large support system in place to assist in all our challenges and realize all our dreams. All we need to do is ask! If we remember we are spiritual beings this will make connection with your guides easier. But if we forget or don't know we are spiritual beings and identify with our egos instead we consequently have a lower vibration and a more distant frequency range from the spirit world making it harder to connect.

NOTES

The good news is that no matter what your vibration or frequency is, if you want to connect with your guides and benefit from their support you can. All you need to do is first connect with your own spirit and the simplest way to do this is to recognize what makes you come alive. What inspires you, gives you strength, fortifies and nourishes you at the core of your being, leaves you feeling satisfied, in love with love and comfortable in your own skin. These are ways to connect yourself with your own spirit. The closer you are to your unique self the closer you are to your guides, as they vibrate on your same frequency. If you're not connected or not sensitive to your spirit, chances are very high you will be disconnected to any assistance your guides offer. The more you pay attention to what you want and love, the more you will sense your guides assisting in your success. They do everything possible to make your life easier, happier, and satisfying if you ask them to. In respecting your free will, they cannot interfere with your life, change your decisions, or change your path. They can only assist your decisions and support them and your unique spirit and deepest happiness. Do you know how eager your guides are to assist you? Just ask them, the more you ask of them, the more they give and the more they want to serve you. If you want to experience blessings from your guides, ask them to give you a present today. I will guarantee that, before the end of the day, you will receive one and they enjoyed doing it for you. Don't struggle any more in life than you have to. Life is challenging enough, this is why our Divine Source gave us a support system. So open your hearts and let your guides in, they love you and are eager to assist you in anyway. There are those in spirit life whose mission is to help and guide us in our earthly existence. They are noble personalities of good intent. There is probably much truth in contention that your guides are attracted to humans where there exist a common bond; that is of "like to like." For example, one who possesses an inherent appreciation of harmony, a spirit nurse or doctor would endeavor to influence one who has the latent gift of healing.

NOTES

Others have a devotional purpose, some a scientific approach, and so it is generally so that the guide for an individual is one who has a mutual interest. Guides are lovable and patient people, though times, they may be rather eager to seek all possible occasions to influence their human charge. That is why it has been stressed that the matter of self-discipline is very important so your guide knows that they should only draw close into the medium's orbit when he/she is invited to do so. You must remember that your guide needs to learn how and when to use their medium, just as the latter has to learn how to seek attunement with their guides, and submit him or herself to their guide's usage of him/her. It may well be your guide has to content him or herself with using his/her medium as the medium expects him or herself to be used in this connection, it is the medium's mind that is the dominate factor; for it is recalled that it is the medium's conscious and sub-conscious mental equipment that is employed by the guide. Therefore, should it be that a beginner, possibly through ill-informed leadership or copying others, feels that their guide should speak in broken English; they will be content to tolerate the weakness, as a means to an end. The purest form of mediumship to be desired is that when your guide becomes as second nature to a medium, so that they can project their thoughts intuitively in to the Third-Eye of the medium's consciousness, without a state of trance being necessary at all. There is a common statement "Your guides will not let you down." This is, of course, very true, but we should not impose upon your guides responsibilities beyond their power to perform. No guide is omnipotent. They, like us, can only deal with the material they have. They can direct good influencing, give thought directives, guide us to good motives, within their capacity of comprehending our problems. You should not expect them to prevent one from slipping on a banana skin, catching a cold when you are soaked through from the elements, win the lottery, find a home to live in, or direct customers to one's business.

NOTES

A student should avoid "guide worship" and "it's my guide that says this or that." Let us see them as they really are. They have fine personalities, more advanced in wisdom than ourselves, but who have their limitations as we have. The biggest limitation in mediumship is ourselves. We all respond to the laws governing cause and effect, and your guides cannot alter this. Your guides cannot foresee your physical future very far ahead. They can, however, influence your minds, give you thought directives, inspire you, and give you inner strength of purpose. At times they can foresee immediate danger and help you to avoid it. They can assist you to overcome the ill-effect of sickness, and to cultivate your virtues. You should regard them with affection and confidence, as that of a big brother or sister, but knowing this, you should avoid expecting them to fulfill functions that are outside their province. Not only do you need to know your spirit guides, but you also need to acquaint yourself with your archangels and elementals as well. I will describe them and give you a briefing of how they assist you everyday, all you have to do is call upon them at any hour of your day. There are seven archangels that sit with the Divine Source.

NOTES

<u>RAPHAEL</u> (Rah-Fay-EL,) Raphael stands on a hill in front of you. Raphael is dressed in a yellow robe with purplish highlights with an emerald-green aura around him. He carries a caduceus wand (the symbol used by MD's, a wand entwined by serpents, which represents life force). Raphael's robe waves in the wind. You should feel his breeze coming from behind him. Raphael comes in from the East and brings us regenerative life force from Divine Source. His name means "God is Healing." He journeys on the wings of the wind and acts as the bearer of Divine Source's love to mankind. His healing comes in the form of knowledge or energy that restores us to wholeness. He is thought to wear a tablet engraved with the Divine Source's name, and his symbol is a serpent. Raphael is one of seven holy angels who seats at the throne of Divine Source. He rules over the second level of the Other Side. He is first seen curing Tobit's blindness with a salve of ash from the burnt bladder of a fish. For this reason he is often shown carrying a fish. He is one of "the Watchers," and one who is set over the diseases and wounds of humanity. He heals the earth and furnishes a habitat for man. He is the Guardian of the Tree of Life, and holds a medical book describing all the healing substances Infinite Spirit has given to mankind. He is also known as the Angel of the Sun, and as the Angel of Science and Knowledge. Turn to Raphael when you are ill at any level. His gifts comes in many forms, including herbs, plants, and the knowledge of color. He encourages you to look within, and to mend any sense of separation from the source, the casual factor in all diseases. He blesses healers, MD's, nurses, and all who offer their talents and gifts in the art of healing. He helps heal your physical challenges in yourself and others. Raphael also wants you to know you are a healer like he is. Raphael surrounds physical ailments with healing energy of emerald green-light; this energy is absorbed where needed. He speaks to healers through their thoughts and feelings. If your life purpose is to be a healer he can help you know what areas of healing to study and assist with all aspects in your healing career. Raphael's twinflame is Mother Mary.

NOTES

__GABRIELLE__ (Gab-ray-EL,) Gabrielle stands behind you, dressed in blue with orange highlights with a crimson aura around him. Gabrielle holds a cup and is surrounded by waterfalls. Take notice to the feel of moisture in the air when he is present. Gabrielle comes in from the south and is the second-highest-ranking angel. His name means "God is my strength," he is the messenger of Divine comfort. Gabrielle is the Angel of the Annunciation, who revealed to the Blessed Virgin Mary that she would bear a child who would be the son of Divine Source. He is also known as the Angel of Resurrection, of Mercy, Vengeance, Death, and Revelation. Gabrielle rules over Paradise, the first level on the Other Side. He sits on the left-hand side of Divine Source. Gabrielle is credited with great miracles in all traditions. In the testimony of Joan of Arc, it was he who appeared to her and inspired her to go to the aid of the King of France. He is also thought to be the Angel of the Moon, who brings mankind the gift of hope. Gabrielle represents the word of Divine Source and symbolizes the essence of our highest truth. Turn to him whenever you are faced with the need to speak out about things you know and feel to be right. He assists all those who speak publicly and teach higher truths, such as writers, teachers, actors, priests, and healers. He brings healing to the higher centers of your mind. Gabrielle assists you if your life purpose is in the arts or communication. He helps polish and trust in your natural talents, and then opens doors for you to express these talents in a way to help others. All he needs from you is honesty and cooperation. Tell him about your fears, your hopes, your confusion, your insecurities, and your dreams. Ask him to help you, and then walk through the doors of opportunity that he has opened for you. He is on your side completely! His function is to be your coach and to prod you along. Please know that he is only pushing you along because he knows you need a boost from above. Gabrielle's twinflame is Archeia Hope, everyone has a twinflame.

NOTES

MICHAEL (Mee-chai-EL,) to your right stands Michael dressed in scarlet with green highlights with a cyan blue aura around him. Michael holds a flaming sword; you should feel the heat coming from this direction. Michael comes in from the west. Michael is the most powerful angel, revered equally in most religions. His name means "Who is as God," his position on the Other Side is on the right of the Throne of Glory, and on earth at the right hand of man. Archangel Michael is chief of all the Archangels and head of all the angelic order of Virtues and ruler of the fourth heaven. Michael is the conqueror of evil and the defender of our integrity. He is Divine Source's great messenger of live and mercy, who leads the souls of the just to the Other Side. He is well known to have announced to Sarah that she would give birth to Isaac, preventing the sacrifice of Jacob, later wrestled with Jacob, and led the Israelites during their wandering in the wilderness. Michael is the Prince of Light in the Dead Sea scroll known as "The Wars of the Sons of Light against the Sons of Darkness." He is seen as forerunner of the Shekhinah (Bride of Divine Source), and as the angel of the burning bush. Michael told the Virgin Mary of her approaching assumption. He sheds his tears over the sinful that are faithful, and combined to form the cherubim. He asks you to bring harmony and order into your lives, to avoid chaos as an invitation to evil, and to live in accordance with our highest principles. As old years give way to new, Michael enables us to release outworn ideas and stale resentments, so we can move on into the new years ahead unburdened by anything that will weigh our spirit down. He is with you giving you the courage to make life changes that will help you work toward your divine life purpose. Since we are all Light Workers, he is overseeing the fruition of your Divine life be assured you are never alone, and will never be alone. When you feel a push to make changes at work or at home, this is Michael's influence, encouraging you to make your life purpose a high priority, Ask Michael to help, and it is done with his twinflame Faith.

NOTES

<u>URIEL</u> (Yhr-ree-El) to your left visualize Uriel dressed in greens and browns on a fertile landscape. She holds some sheaves of wheat. Uriel leads the angelic armies, and stands before the Throne of Glory on the Other Side. Her name means "Light of God," she represents the light of Divine Source teaching. Uriel is synonymous with our passion to unite with the Source. She is called the Flame of God, the Angel of the Presence, and Archangel of Salvation. She is known to chastise Moses, and parted the Red Sea. She illuminated Ezra's prophetic visions and watches over thunder and terror. Uriel is seen as the Angel of Repentance, and is thought to be the Prince of Lights referred to in one of the Dead Sea scrolls. Uriel is the angel who guarded the gates of Eden with a fiery sword, and guided Abraham out of Ur, and gave men the knowledge of Alchemy and the Kabbalah. Her name is inscribed on amulets to help them in their study of their higher self. Uriel's energy is radiant, and is believed in some occult circles to be the antidote to radiation. She is portrayed symbolically as an open hand holding a sheaf of wheat, and offer mankind the gift of enlightenment, which is the realization of Divinity within oneself. Uriel is called the "Psychologist Angel, because she helps heal toxins from people's thoughts and emotions. She is especially able to release stubborn anger and unforgiving. She is with you right now to clear away such toxins. Uriel would like to work with you to help others clear away their emotional and psychological blocks. Her healing work is subtle, and never forces it on anyone. She believes that it is best to wait until you approach her and directly request guidance or assistance. Then she simply and lovingly asks you to be willing to release toxins from your mind and heart. If you are willing to do so then the release will occur. Uriel chooses to wait so you retain your dignity and control, while choosing to be cleared of lower energies. Uriel's twinflame is Aurora, I'll go into more detail of twinflames in our next chapter.

NOTES

METATRON *(Met-Ta-Tron) Metatron and Sandalphon are twins and the tallest Archangels, extending from heaven to Earth with their continuity of Sacred Services from heaven; to carry human prayers to the Divine to be answered. Metatron, on earth he was the Prophet Enoch, who was taken up to the Other Side and transformed into an Angel of Fire with thirty-six pairs of wings. He appears as an enormous being of brilliant White Light, and the greatest of all the Hierarchy on the Other Side. He is the Master of the Highest Power of Abundance, chancellor and King of the Angels on the Other Side. Metatron's twin brother, Sandalphon, the Prophet Elijah on earth; both with names not ending with "el", both were the only two Archangels who were mortal men upon the Earth. The Divine gave both men their immortal assignments as Archangels to reward them for their good work on Earth, allowing them to continue their Sacred Services from heaven. Elijah/Sandalphon's ascension occurred when he was lifted up to heaven in a fiery chariot pulled by two horses of fire, accompanied by a whirlwind, and even recorded in the second chapter of the Book of 2 Kings. Sandalphon's assignment is to assist expected parents in knowing to sex of their child and entering music into the souls of mankind.*

SARIEL *(Sar-ree-El) this seraph is given the role of deciding the fate of angels who stray from the path of the Divine Source. Sariel is also the Angel of Death. He was a healer like Raphael, a Seraphim and the Prince of Presence. Sariel is also credited as being an Angel of Knowledge and one of the leaders of the armies on the Other Side. His name was written on shields of one of the fighting forces. Sariel was, in fact, one of the fallen rebel angels.*

NOTES

EVIL ORIGIN

<u>LUCIFER</u> (Loo-see-Fer) most beloved by Infinite Spirit and sadly a fallen angel, whose ambitions were a distortion of the Infinite Spirit's plans. He is known to us through various religious teachings as the fallen angel, with the use of many names such as; Satan, Belial, Beelzebub, and the Devil. Because of the variety of teachings we have come to "untruth" when it comes to this most beautiful of Angels whose name means "Bearer of the Light". In his original Glory as Samuel, highest and above seraphim, with twelve radiant wings, outshone all other Angels until one day our Divine Source and Samuel had a heated discussion about how man should live upon the earth plane. The Divine wanted man, while on the earth plane to make soulfulness and enlightenment top priority and to maintain close contact with Divine Source and have the knowledge that the Divine does. Samuel/Lucifer, wanted man to make maintaining the earth their top priority and to have little knowledge for fear that man would over rule the heavens. This insecurity led to the battles in heaven. Divine felt that these insecurities would lead to the seven deadly sins such as: Pride, Envy, Anger, Lust, Greed, Gluttony, and Sloth. There are seven other legends studied in Angelogy, we will never really know for sure what happen, but here are the other seven legends. The fist legend is that there was a shadow side of God, the separation of the good side from the bad side is now established and the fall is complete. The second legend is your free will, because angels had the free will to leave the Divine Unity, the fallen angels chose to leave. The third legend was Lust, the strong urges and seduction of Adam's daughters, then took them as wives. The fourth legend was Pride, the angel were cast out because of audacity thinking that he was higher than thee. The fifth legend was war; angels were created with free will and were fallible. The first sets of angels were created on the second day of creation, but God was very uncomfortable with the idea that his creations could sin, so he strengthened them with grace.

NOTES

He then created a second group of angels but withheld grace and so gave them the opportunity to sin; they embraced the sin with enthusiasm. The sixth legend was passion of the redeemer, God gave them the power to tempt, test, and finally punish mankind. So instead of abandoning us, God took human form, as Jesus, to make reconciliation with his creations. Lucifer transgressed the terms of the contract because he baited and hooked god for breaking the contract which states that only Lucifer had dominion over the sinner on the earth plane. When Lucifer tried to siege Jesus' soul, the trap was sprung, it was God instead. The seventh legend was disobedience, when God created angels he told them to bow to no one but himself. Then God created Adam whom God considered higher than the angels. Then he commanded the angels to bow before the new figure, forgetting his previous commandment. Lucifer refused because partly he couldn't disobey the first commandment, and also he would only bow to his beloved God. God didn't understand Lucifer's dilemma and just thought he was being disobedient and cast him out of heaven. "Lucifer stated to overcome evil one has to have evil to overcome, came to the earth plane to supply the evil, this was an agreement between Lucifer and the Divine, to have mankind grow spiritually through all the trials and tribulation within evil; becoming strong enough to conquer these evil aspects that are thrown in our way as tests for spiritual growth, spiritual advancement and a oneness with the Divine."

NOTES

The summary to the previous page is not that I'm protecting or excusing the evil, What I am trying to explain is that you have to credit some of your spiritual growth to some of the evil in the world and know how amazing you really are to overcome such negative powers. Even Lucifer has a twinflame, Vessel Lucy.

EARTH BEINGS

<u>MANKIND</u> before enlightenment can happen for man, events must happen. This must happen so man can judge for themselves, their future before the "Day of Fire." It will cleanse the world from what has been done to it over thousands of years. Pertaining to the "Day of Fire," mentioned in the Bible, Mathew 24, verses 34-36, about a man standing and others are disappearing. God promises to protect anyone individual who believes in him by surrounding whomever with (3) Angelic Figures, (9) feet tall, (6) feet wide. The (9) is for the power of enlightenment, (3) threefold, (6) is three times the norm. This represents the makeup of man at this time of life span. Man has become their own worst enemy and the Beast of the Earth. The number (6) stands for imperfection of man in the eyes of God and all spiritually inclined individuals. In Revelations, chapter 13, verse 18. "This calls for wisdom, if anyone has insight, let him calculate the numbers of the Beast, for it is man's number, the number 666."

<u>WALK-INS</u> the process of walk-ins is simply that the body is used by more than one soul in order to accomplish what the soul wants to accomplish. This agreement usually happens prior to the body being born. Keep clear in your mind that the body is like a suit of clothes a soul will wear in a lifetime. You get them, use them, discard them and then you get new ones. Another type of walk-ins is when someone goes through life and their free will doesn't foul things up too badly, they actually reach a point, earlier than expected, where they have accomplished everything they came to accomplish. So now they need to decide to leave early.

NOTES

Which if all their contractual agreements have been met within their, "web of souls" then they are free to leave. At this point they can choose to tackle other things from other lifetimes or just leave. If they decide to leave, sometimes they are approached by another soul, on what you call their higher level, to see if this soul can come and take up residence. It may be to take care of just a couple of loose ends or it might be to get several things tied up. And again, they make the switch. The major difference here is that the incoming soul has not preprogrammed anything into the body and usually ends up having to work within at least some minor restrictions. Let's say the secondary soul is going to come, plan for a total different person in that relationship. One day you wake up and your lying by this person you thought was your spouse. You get as usual, they look the same, but their attitude toward things is a little different from the day before. Don't get alarmed, they are from the same soul group, they just have different ways of doing things, and because they are from a higher level, they are most of the time a better person. Walk-in is an ancient concept first described in Hinduism whose modern name originated in the Spiritualist faith and was popularized by the related, but not identical New Age movements and beliefs. A walk-in is thought to be a person whose original soul has departed his/her body and been replaced with a new soul. Walk-ins first appeared in Hindu sacred literature. In Hindu belief, each person is comprised of several bodies, including the physical, astral, mental, refined, and so on. The only essence that is <u>not</u> a body, and therefore not transferable, is the Divine (Supreme Spirit.) So according to this belief system, a walk-in, by merging, can take one or many of these bodies. The most famous story of a walk-in is that of the missionary of Hinduism was Saint Tirumular. Legend has it that he voluntarily left his body in order to reanimate a young cow herder who had just died. His own body was subsequently taken up to heaven by the god Siva, leaving him to spend the remainder of his life on earth in the body of the cow herder.

NOTES

This cow herder was able to access the missionary's knowledge, including his ability to speak in foreign tongue of Tamil. In modern times; a typical walk-in involves an individual (frequently, but not always, female) who is badly injured, falls ill or is in some way incapacitated, or seems to "die" on the operating table during surgery, perhaps later reporting a near-death experience. Others claim that deep emotional trauma and suicidal desires alone may set the stage for a walk-in experience. After resuscitation, the person may believe in a manner completely at odds with earlier, established behavior patterns. He/she may speak in an unknown language and identify by a different name, and may be frightened and confused, or supernal calm. While the experience can not be determined to have any objective reality, subjectively it is deeply and importantly real for the affected individual. Invariably, a walk-in will state they either do not know where the original inhabitant of the body has gone to, or the original soul has left it and has gone to the other side, or reincarnated, etc., leaving them in charge. The new individual may claim he/she is an angel; a "new" version of the former self; an older, more experienced soul; less often, a brand new one who has never incarnated before; or any manner of other origins. Many walk-ins claim heightened psychic sensitivity and may take up work as New Age healers or ministers. Other claim inability to accomplish basic tasks of daily living, for some, may have a number of secondary gains. While this belief system about walk-ins claims that these transitions can not occur involuntarily and that no soul walks into another's body without reason, the behavior of some "new" people indicates that it may not always be so. In classical cases, the change is immediately apparent. However, in cases where the "new soul" has enough information to take up life of the "previous occupant" seamlessly, it takes weeks or months before a walk-in notices, or becomes to believe, that a transition has indeed occurred.

NOTES

Occasionally, the "old self" returns after a period of months or years, and either the "new self" departs, or they coexist and may try to integrate into a single being, or work out means of cooperation and live as two persons in one body. In 1979 a renowned Spiritualist brought the concept of walk-ins to the attention of the general public. Shortly after a belief system grew around walk-in experiences, complete with all the usual attributes such as "ascending into higher frequencies of evolution", predictions regarding earth changes, and the concept that the new person may possess a variety of psi powers (of Black Masses) unknown to ordinary human beings whose "vibrational levels" remain unraised. This new walk-in belief system includes a number of variant experiences such as channeling, telepathy contact with extraterrestrial intelligences, or soul merging, where the original soul is said to remain present, coexisting or integrating with the new one. As of 2006, an increasing number of people claim some type of walk-in experience. Walk-ins were featured on unsolved mysteries in 1999. According to information presented on this program, there are now walk-in conventions, one of them drawing approximately 500 people.

I have included a checklist to determine a walk-in status:

- *Name changes*
- *Career changes*
- *New interest in the study of psychic phenomena*
- *A feeling that one is not really from earth*
- *A sudden desire to move to a new environment*
- *Memory loss*
- *Sudden onset of allergic reactions*

Since all of these factors could possibly be attributed to simple life changes such as adolescence or middle age, it's difficult to determine solely from my checklist if a "true" walk-in has occurred.

NOTES

The most logical method would be to determine if any specific event historically connected with walk-ins (anesthesia for surgery is one of the most common) occurred around the time one first started feeling differently. All souls come to the earth in order to accomplish missions of cosmic significance, and that a walk-in is a highly evolved soul who is here to help raise vibrational levels of humanity and doesn't want to bother with the tedious process of incarnating in the usual fashion (i.e., birth). Walk-ins are not perfect like Ascended Masters, but are invariably more spiritual, compassionate and sympathetic than the original person. This interpretation is sometimes disputed by spouses of people who abruptly discontinue marital relations on the grounds that they are not the person whose name appears on the wedding license or that carnal love is not for those of higher vibrational frequencies. Separation, divorce, and remarriage are very common in a walk-in experience.

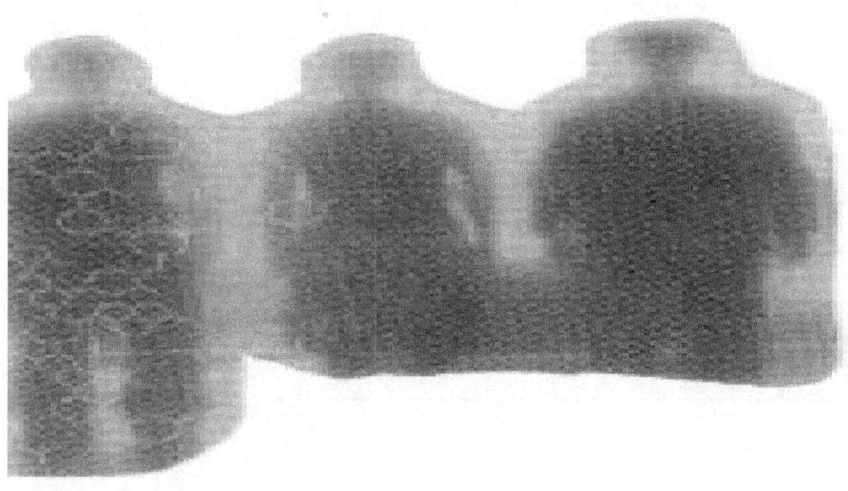

NOTES

ASTRAL BODY this is a manifestation of the spiritual aspect of a living entity, (identical twin of yourself.) Again, it is always attached to an incarnate being. When detached, it quickly moves to higher planes of existence in order to reincarnate. In this unattached condition they are too busy to occupy your time. When attached to some individual ego, they can be seen as such. Higher Spiritual Entities are not linked to a particular ego.

ETHERIC BODY is an emanation of all created things. It is not the true astral double and is something like "halfway between astral and physical." It sometimes can take on the appearance of a person on a higher plane, but is always attached to a living being.

ELEMENTALS (lowest dominator in spirit,) these are a special type of spirit, having a special association with one of the four elements.

ARTIFICIAL ELEMENTALS are entities created by human forces and are composed of only one element. They are focused toward one purpose, so if you leave them alone they will ignore you. Depending upon the strength of will of their creator, they will appear more or less gaunt when seen on the Astral Plane.

EMPTY ONES If you live in a large city, these entities can be seen in physical form in the "skid row" section of town. They look human, but they have no soul and no hope for the future. They can sometimes show great humor and daring, but quickly fade into the depths of despair. Their eyes show either madness or emptiness. These poor creatures also exist on higher planes. Their touch brings despair and fear.

LARVAE these are known as lemurs. It is believed that they live off the essence of blood. They "feed," so to speak, on sick or injured people. They can be dispersed easily by a projection of pure spiritual white light.

LILITH (rules over pixie land,) she is a winged female demon of the night who steals children at or before child s birth and visits men in their sleep. She was Adam's mistress prior to wife of Satan.

NOTES

<u>GHOSTS'</u> ghosts and haunting do exist, in fact they're more common than you think. The average ghosts are generally harmless. They can be healed and removed from any location quite easily. Because there is no room or space for limitations in the spiritual realm, a knowledgeable psychic healer can rid a home of a ghost by either visiting the location or through distant healing. When most of us die, our soul, which looks like a little ball of light, leaves the physical body and briefly enters the astral plane which is a spiritual way station. While in the astral plane a person's soul might float around its earthly body for awhile, or it might check in on certain relatives to say good-bye, until it finally realizes it is dead. Usually, at that point the soul feels itself being drawn into the White Light of Infinite Spirit's loving healing energy. A ghost is nothing more than a soul who remains on the astral plane, instead of going into the White Light as it should. The primary reason ghosts remain on the astral plane is because they don't realize they're dead. Another reason so many ghosts exist is because many of us don't believe in life after death. When the soul separates from the body, it seems too many that are still alive. After all they can still see and hear the people around them. However, when they try to communicate with the living, and we don't respond these same souls often become very confused, frustrated, and lonely. Since people are not taught to go into the light to be cleansed and healed, they often mistake their focus on their former earthly possessions, friends, and families who are alive. Unfortunately causes them to remain on the astral plane. To understand the ghostly realm one has to realize that time is very different on the astral plane. One hundred years in earth time seems like just a few months on the astral plane. Since many ghosts stay attached to a home or building for several hundred years, they're periodically forced to deal with new families moving in and out of their home. It's no wonder inhabiting ghosts sometimes get upset and "haunt" us.

NOTES

<u>PSEUDO-GHOSTS'</u> these are not related to true ghosts. They're closer to little nasties (pixies.) They "feed" off any energy given to them and will imitate the actions of ghosts in order to get people to pay attention and give them energy. By reading the Astral Light they can know your past and probable future, and thus may appear at séances under the guise of a deceased loved one. They are more bothersome on the physical plane than on any higher plane.

<u>DYING</u>

We all are too familiar with this process, but you really have to examine it clearly. We should be very eager to die, I'm not saying to go and commit suicide, but don't be so fearful about it. You've heard the word disposable, almost everything we touch today is disposable, including our bodies. Picture yourself as an automobile that just cannot run anymore. You bring it to the dealer to get a new one or just send it to the junkyard and dispose of it. You enter the junkyard, get out of your car; (you as your soul and the car being your physical body) and all is left is your soul. You're definitely not going to allow yourself to be shrunk into that small block of metal nor do you need the can anymore. So you walk away from it. Your soul is pure energy that never dies. You don't die when you drop off your car; only the car/ physical body is disposed of.

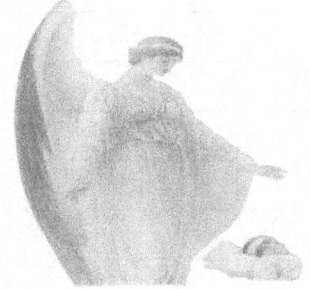

NOTES

BETWEEN LIVES

The length of time spent between lives may vary, depending on your life lessons and their integration from your previous lessons, also preparation for your next life. While between lives you may be involved in helping spirits here on earth. You know you need to advance and develop in this life, you are expected to do so between lives as well. You've heard of Spirit Guides and wondered if they exist. Well they do, they are spirit always watching over less developed spirit on earth. If we need to advance or develop, we may do this between lives. Since time does not exist in the between-times and to watch over an earth-bound spirit for its earthly lifetime would not actually hinder you as a watcher's progress. In fact, it would add to it in the sense of gaining "student-teacher" experience.

REINCARNATION

Reincarnation is an ancient belief. It is part of many religions and was even one of the original Christian tenets, until condemned by the Second Council of Constantinople in 553 C.E. It is believed that the human spirit, or soul, is a fragment of the divine and eventually will return to its divine source. But, for its own evolution, it is necessary that your soul experience all things in life. It is sensible and logically explainable of why one is born into a rich family and another very poor. Why should one be born crippled, another fit and strong. It is because we must all experience all things. For someone who does not believe in reincarnation, it is hard for them to understand the death of a child. It is because the child has learned all that had been set to be learned in that particular lifetime and so was moving on. A very good example for this is the grades of school. You enter school in a low grade and learn the basics. When you have mastered these you graduate, take a short vacation, then come back into a higher grade and experience more things. So as it is in earth life. To come back into a higher grade you are reborn in a new body.

NOTES

Occasionally, you will remember parts of a previous life, but more generally you do not. It is possible to be induced into a past life by hypno-regression. Then there is the experience of de'ja`-vu the feeling this has happened before, this is the most evidence we can have for reincarnation. When we reincarnate we will be human once again, as well as animals of all kinds, they will return as they are not into another animal. The reason for this is the balance of nature. However you may reincarnate as the opposite sex to experience that side of you. Do not ever forget you are of both genders, male and female.

ASTRAL PROJECTION

Most of us feel uncomfortable with the idea of Astral Projection, but you shouldn't because you do it every time you daydream, and very frequently when you dream in sleep. Astral Travel, which follows Astral Projection, is also very common and natural. In fact, you probably had to unlearn how to Astral Travel when you were a child. It was very common for your parents to tell you not to play in invisible scenes and with invisible playmates. These were scenes and entities on and from the Astral Plane. Your parents would say, "Come back to reality!" "Don't play foolish games!" And, worst of all, "Quit pretending," it was eventually impressed into your conscious to forget those invisibles which are "see-able" on the Astral Plane. This process of elimination would make you uncomfortable or unacceptable to your current state of consciousness and is what most psychotherapists call "motivated forgetting." It is one of the reasons why most people remember little of their infancy; it was so childish and embarrassing not to be able to walk, communicate, take care of yourself or even control your bowels that you want to forget. This book in its entirety will teach you to get back what was taken from you as a child. This is your birth rite, if this gift was not to exist, then why were we born with it.

NOTES

CLOSENESS BETWEEN PHYSICAL AND SPIRIT MIND

The ability to distinguish between thought from self and that which comes from spirit was very hard to determine in earlier days. It is a very delicate adjustment. The reason for this is that your consciousness is sensitive to what your Third-Eye portrays whether it emanates from self or literal spirit. The two can merge into each other, with the strong probability that at first the physical mind will predominate. For example, if a picture is received in the Third-Eye from spirit, and perceived by the conscious mind, then the latter will naturally begin to question it and ask "what is this?" This uncertainty presents a developing medium with initial difficulties, but there are ways in which authenticity of spirit communication can be judged. A picture received from spirit is very vivid and makes such a strong impression on the consciousness that it can be revived easily at any time. Try to build up a picture in your mind of a common object, say, your favorite book. If this is compared with a spirit vision it will not even approach the vividness of the latter. The spirit picture will be permanent and can be recalled in a flash, whereas it will take a conscious effort to build up the picture of your book. When a flow of thought is received from a spirit source, which the conscious automatically converts into words, there will be a great impulse to speak them. The student will be able to hold them back, but it will need an effort to do so, and the insistence behind the desire to speak will be so considerable that you will have the inner-knowledge that the thoughts are not of your own creation. The difference between this and the seeking of normal thought is usually so marked that the student will not question its origin. Sometimes a student to mediumship may gather from conversations with mediums or in witnessing their mediumship that the reception of spirit communication needs a form of sensational preparation and sensitivity-that may well be out of true perspective with reality. Communication is a natural and simple act that follows attunement with spirit.

NOTES

Every medium, especially clairvoyants and clairaudients, know that in order to receive communication from spirit they first need to place their minds into a condition of receptive abandonment. In other words, they will need to clear the Third-Eye in their minds of mundane thoughts to allow the incoming vision or sound to register. An example of this is, when a person receives an inspirational thought "out of the blue," or sees a vision, it is quite unexpected, these come when the person's mind "is not thinking of anything," and that simply means the Third-Eye is clear at the moment to allow the incoming spirit impression to be received. In early days of development one should sit only the regular circle times arranged for. The student should never sit for control alone. They should only sit in the presence of an experienced medium in the proper circle. When sitting the primary purpose should be that through meditation leading to the surrender of the physical consciousness so your spirit-mind will be able to rise above, and convey impressions to your Eye of the mind, which the student registers. The student must be willing for their guides to communicate through him/her. Because no mind can ever become blank, the student is advised to sit comfortably, resignedly, then to gently meditate upon some spiritual train of thought, letting their mind enter into a state which can best be described as "day-dreaming." In doing this there should be a spiritual objective. There can be the gentle contemplation of beautiful things, flowers, a garden, seeking healing for the sick, seeking a way to show humanity the way of redemption. Your inner-self should be willing for the inflow of thought or pictures to come from a higher spiritual nature, as it comes, then subconsciously you should welcome it, and just let it flow continuously. This way your mind becomes quiet, gently letting the condition of receptivity to rise for the thought-pictures to register themselves from spirit. There is no sudden break from one phase to another; it is gentle, smooth merging of good thought intention from the medium's meditation to the incoming thought from spirit sources.

NOTES

It can be linked to two streams of thought that merge together. There is no dividing line between the two. It is in this manner that communication first comes and projects itself within the Eye of the mind so that your consciousness is aware of the inflow of thought from the student's spirit guides.

MEDITATION IS KEY TO SELF DISCIPLINE

It is vitally essential as a medium you must always be master of yourself. You should only sit for development at the prescribed times. You must not sit for control alone. If at any other time you feel the presence of your guides with you, you must not allow them to become dominant. You should set out the mental instruction "not them, and only when you invite them." If they become dominant you should immediately turn their thought into other directions and occupy yourself with other things. In the eagerness of the early days when your guides' presence commences to be felt in the developing circle, it was natural for a student to wish their development to enhance more quickly, and at times their guides desired this too. It is, however, best to develop slowly, yet progressively, and on no account should any encouragement be given for control or trance conditions to come except on the special occasions arranged for this under the leadership of the circle leader. The rule should be firmly established, that there must be an invitation extended to the guide, before they enters into the medium's orbit. This particularly applies to automatic writing, which will be dealt with in a later chapter. Sometimes when a student is resting, his mind is at ease, the desire to write will come. This must be resisted, for otherwise the practice will over-run discretion and the medium becomes addicted to it far more than they should. I don't mean to repeat myself, but, a medium must always be master of him self, especially in early development, to avoid their mediunship becoming a nuisance to their selves or others, and building a habit that may be hard to break.

NOTES

As a rule developing circles are held only once a week and this should be the only time definite contact with your guides is sought for. This occasion should be looked forward to, and anticipated with calm eagerness, and it must be restrained to that occasion alone. Your guide will, of course, always be with their medium, to give good influence and to protect them in all ways that are possible, but this service can be given without the need for a medium to feel their personal presence with them. It is known in some developing circles; various preliminary preparations and restrictions are advised. Some of these suggest that students should fast before sitting, that entirely fresh clothes should be worn, rubber soles on shoes are vetoed on the grounds that rubber will insulate the student from attunement and the student should not sit with crossed arms, but sit with hands outstretched, palms upwards in a supplicate attitude, and so receive "power." It is recalled that mediumship is an outcome of the use of the medium's mental equipment by their guides, one may question these observances. For example, it is good for the student to be at ease and comfortable, as he is more likely to be so if they are not hungry. On the other hand, a heavy meal beforehand is to be avoided. In spite of what I just said, and the further statements to follow, so long as a student is content to sit in a developing circle that advises these restrictions, etc. they should accept them and not put up any opposition which would destroy the harmony of the circle. If they feel out of harmony with the circle procedure, etc., it would be advisable for them to leave with good grace. In the East, a way of development is to subdue the body into a state of inertia, by atonement, continual exercise, fasting and continuous repetitive intonations, each of these having the objective of so weakening the mental resistance that control can be established through weakness. To use our image of the Third-Eye, the purpose is to thoroughly tire the normal consciousness, so that spirit impressions can occupy happily, this does not apply in modern or western practices which follows more enlightened methods based upon a clear understanding of psychic science.

NOTES

This method takes the view that it is best for the student to be contented and comfortable, so that they are more easily able to let their mind become relaxed and free, and so allow their awareness of their guide's influence to reach them in a natural and normal way. Wearing of rubber shoes cannot affect attunement with you guide. The idea that it can do, arises from the mistaken impression held by some people that it is necessary to be "grounded" with the earth because development follows the magnetic theory of polarization; so if the shoes are left off, the magnetic contact comes more easy. If we consider this in the light of our fundamental postulate that contact with your guides is of the mind, then magnetic forces (which are physical forces) can have no effect. In any case it is apparent that a spirit radiation can permeate any physical material, and because rubber provides an insulation again electrical force, it is no reason why it must be an insulated of a non-physical spirit force. The advice against crossing your arms can only have a psychological basis; it can bring out a state of establishment. Common-sense tells you that no positioning of your body, arms or hands impede attunement, though it can have a psychological value. Vibration is a word that is commonly used in psychic circles for example, "your guide comes in on a certain vibration." There are "cross-vibrations," and so forth. This word is often used loosely and sometimes without supporting reasons. We all know that all matter is a form of characteristic vibration or radiation; and this equally applies to "thought." It is a true statement that for your reception of radiation there must exist, a state of harmony or conductorship between the transmitter and the receiver. In trance and intuitive mediumship it is the transmission of thought radiations that are received from your guides by the medium's Third-Eye. This is the only "vibration" which matters. It is true that different thought directives can set up different vibrations, and if these impinge within your Third-Eye at the same time, then confusion is created. This can be understood by comparison, that if two people are speaking at the same time the listener is unable to comprehend either.

NOTES

It is enough that when a student is seeking communication from their guides, it is their guide's thought force that is invited, and there should be no other. No mind can be occupied with two purposeful thought directives at the same time, and therefore it is impossible for a medium to receive two thought directives from two different spirit personalities, simultaneously. When you are in a conversation within a psychic circle, there are talks about "cross vibrations" and this is considered in the light of possibilities, any such difficulty that arises from this is very remote. This remoteness can be put into its right perspective when you consider how hard it is to impinge your thoughts onto another. It is said that when any two people differ in thought that cross vibrations are created; there is no harm in this, indeed it is your right to hold individual opinions, otherwise we would be robots, which we are not. When you, as a student begin to sit in a developing circle you should follow out the instructions given by its teacher and submit your mind to the common endeavor of the circle. If this is done, there is no question of cross vibrations. In the event, the student is unable to accept the teacher's instructions or methods then you should withdraw from the circle. Between all students and teachers, there should be a state of happy harmony and full co-operation. Any personal opinions about the student or teacher, or personal problem outside or at home, should be deleted from your mind when entering the circle. The ultimate success of any developing circle largely depends upon a condition of contentment within your circle.

NOTES

CLAIRVOYANCE

Clairvoyance is received two ways, "objective" and "intuitive." First consider objective clairvoyance, when a medium sees a spirit person (or an object) as if it is physically present. He will see the presence the same way as they see an ordinary dimensional person. Your spirit visitor may be standing or sitting in a chair looking physically life like in everyway. Therefore it gives the full impression that it is being seen with your eyes. As a rule, the vision does not last long, perhaps only a second or two, before it fades. The visitor is non-physical, and therefore cannot reflect light for the eyes to observe it. Although it appears a medium sees their vision with their eyes, actually they do not, yet, I have to account for an association between the spirit realm and the realm of matter, for example, the figure appears to be walking on the ground, it is not suspended in mid-air, or they can be seen with their hands resting on the arm of a chair. No one can be positive of how these associations of spirit form with material things are established and it certainly signifies an awareness of earthly things by your spirit visitors. A logical hypothesis is that a medium is able to observe their spirit people in this way, through their spirit eye of their spirit body which conveys the picture into their Third-Eye where their conscious mind observes it. As a rule your memory of such clairvoyant vision is extremely vivid, it can be recalled strongly to mind, at any time. "Objective" clairvoyance is a rear gift, and is merged with intuitive clairvoyance. While there are interesting speculation concerning the process of "seeing" and the study of details associated with this, that a student should not specifically seek objective clairvoyance, it is not a common form of mediumship and usually comes after time from an intuitive reception. "Intuitive" vision is the general kind received through clairvoyance. This means that when a medium is in an attuned state, a thought picture of a person in spirit, or an object, etc., is conveyed through their spirit mind into the Third-Eye, and so to the consciousness.

NOTES

This has already been described with the example of the pencil, however, with the vital differences of an ordinary pencil to an ever sharp mechanical pencil that does not come from memory, but is projected through your spirit source. It is clearly within the power of a spirit person to project a picture, such as facial features into the Third-Eye in a similar way to which we project a photograph on to a screen. If the face projected is to be recognized, it must be "life-like" and precise, bearing the characteristics possessed in earthly life. It must be so clear, as they invariably are, to enable a medium to give a clear-cut description of them to the person for whom it is intended. As a student, the first visions may appear as if they have risen from their imagination. Apart from the fact that their memory of them is more vivid and lasting, it is natural that doubt arises as to whether it is spirit or not. The best test is to seek proof of it by enquiry with those who are present, whether their features are known to anyone. There is always a purpose behind clairvoyant vision, and if a student can sustain the attunement it is most likely that some further signs of evidence will be forthcoming, either in vision or by intuitive thought. For example, their visitor may present to your vision an object that will identify the spirit, or a thought will come and say "I am so and so." While a student is giving their first descriptions they should try to do this without emotion and try to hold the attunement gently, allowing their thought impressions to continue. The ability of a medium who can describe their visions will depend on their power of simple, yet direct, portrayal. This is not easy, as one can judge from an experiment of trying to have a friend name relatives, so described from their personal family album. Simple phrases provide the best way to do this. Avoid imitation of other mediums methods of descriptions. Try to convey the character of their face more, as well as its shape, and describe any distinguishing features, while giving your description, a student will find it best to do this with their eyes closed, to maintain the continuity of their attunement, to permit additional evidence to surface.

NOTES

If they break off attunement they will be in need of help or to spend more time to re-establishing attunement. A medium's success in obtaining acceptance of their clairvoyance depends upon their faithful description of that which they see and no more. Avoid placing your own interpretation of what your vision means. This is an example of an experienced medium giving a very successful, long detailed and very evidential description of a husband in spirit to his wife. Further evidence followed, concerning the family and their interests. The medium then said" he kept ducks," but this was denied. The medium persisted, and so did their denials, the medium was beginning to lose patience and became upset. The medium insisted that this information was correct, than said, "I can see the duck now, with its tail curling upward and over." With these simple words, the wife laughed, and said "Now, I know what you meant, our name was Drake." The medium seeing a duck, put their own incorrect construction upon it, but as this medium described simply what was actually seen, it provided another piece of good evidence that was immediately accepted. At the risk of repetition, it is very important for a student, to seek and maintain affinity with their transmission. At first, you must allow the whole story to unfold before attempting to give a description. A student should be expectant within listening to their subconscious self for their upcoming of thought directives that may give names or situations associated with their visions. This gift of attunement will become more advanced, and continuous, so you will receive a stream of thought impressions. You should not hesitate or question its authenticity; you should simply let your voice speak that which is being given to you, even though these statements may appear to be "far-fetched." If a medium's description and evidence is not recognized or accepted by anyone present, there may be several reasons for this. So often it is found that the person for whom the description is intended has not recalled from their memory this spirit personality. It may be that this spirit communicant has come without their earthly friends being present.

NOTES

It may be that this medium's ability to adequately describe their vision is not efficient enough to convince their listener. Sometimes a person will act defiantly, and will not acknowledge the description deliberately. When this happens a medium must avoid at all costs an attempt to explain it away trying to justify their mediumship. They must shun all "escape" methods by evasive suggestions such as saying "this spirit was a friend of a friend in your school-days" etc. It is far better to say openly, "this spirit has not been acknowledged, therefore I must leave it. Do not say you are sorry, never apologize for your mediumship, please be content in knowing that what you seen were authentic. It is recognized that it is disconcerting for a medium giving clairvoyance in public for their descriptions not to be accepted, even though they may think this lowers their prestige as a medium. "Escape routes" prejudice the standard of mediumship, they are invariably recognized for what they are and no good comes from them. Well know mediums adopt these escape routes on occasion and they are not inspirational. A student should first and foremost seek the highest standard and maintain it always. Most developing mediums have, as their ideal to practice mediumship in public and their eventual success of this will depend on giving true, simple and accurate descriptions, rather than relying on a slick tongue, or platform patterns. If, after giving a description that has been accepted and no other thought message comes, do not manufacture one. It is true that many people like to have some advice or counsel from their love one's in spirit, and this has become a usual practice with clairvoyance. It is not good to lower the standard of your mediumship by pandering to what some people like. Unfortunately, it has become a common practice of mediumship today, to follow on the description of their spirit people, and what positive proof they can give of their identity with possibly a true message, with some originality to the "message" out of a medium's consciousness that means nothing in particular, and can apply to anyone.

NOTES

A student may find, as their affinity and attunement with spirit becomes established, the clairvoyance may take the form of symbolic signs or situations. These signs may be symmetrical in design usually in white light on a dark background (they can be in color as well). They sometimes have a spiritual significance such as, for example, a picture of enlightened people traveling along a good road toward a goal, while others may be blindly seeking the way, off this road, struggling in a morass. If your guide is a preacher, you will find yourself in a mental picture, preaching a wonderful sermon to the multitude. These situations will be very vivid and should be allowed to continue without mental interruption unless the vision should become too unpleasant. In this connection, if any unpleasant thought or picture is received, a student should at once break off the attunement by opening his eyes, taking notice of what is going on within the circle, and so come back to normality. After a short while, you can again seek attunement with the mental request that such unpleasantries must not be repeated. Should, however, there be a repetition, you must come back to normal and wait for the end of this sitting, and discuss your experience with your teacher. Such experiences like these are very rare, and should not be anticipated. As clairvoyance becomes easy for you, the pictures of your guides and other spirits will be projected into our Third-Eye. At first these may be very small, no bigger than a postage stamp, or on the other hand very large like a close-up on a cinema screen. With practice and experience these will be adjusted until the size appears quite normal. Do not create any pictures out of your mind, for that is interference, gently wait for the upcoming vision, with your mind quite free. Back in the olden days, students may take time in forming visions and if at first you see only one or two visions during a sitting, you should be well satisfied. When the circle is over, or at the appropriate time, when your teacher asks the circle members to tell of their experiences, it is advisable to narrate in simple words what has been observed.

NOTES

This not only encourages a medium's powers of accurate descriptions, but it will give you confidence, and at the same time show to the guide what they have received. Remember your guide is also able to observe that which appears in your Third-Eye, for they are attunement with their medium. Development is two-way, the medium's endeavor to seek attunement with their guides and vice versa. Referring to symbols again, if these are seen, tell of them, but do not ask someone else to interpret their meaning. The reason for this is that "some-one" can only give what their mind can offer. Any impressions that the student may receive at this time will be far more accurate. It is best to accept them and wait for an explanation from their guides (possibly by intuitive thought) and leave it at that. It may be, in the commencement, their guides are conveying simple signs and shapes, like globes or triangles, to be the first lessons in their guide's training for their medium to "see." Concerning the messages that accompany clairvoyance, it will be recalled that "thoughts" are not "words." It is through a medium's knowledge of words that their consciousness will interpret these thoughts into a description. A French student who knows no English would receive the same thought radiation as a British, but they would interpret their thought into French words, and the British into English words. Let us again refer to the pencil example. If a spirit visitor wishes to give their thought of a pencil, the consciousness would receive the picture of it, and their medium would know what it intended. This does not mean that all thought descriptions are presented in picture form, but they can be in thought also. This may be more easily understood if you consider that if in conversation the word pencil is used, the consciousness knows what is meant by a sub-conscious picture of it in your Third-Eye. So if in a clairvoyant presentation a spirit visitor wishes to provide evidence of their earth experiences, he may give to their medium's Third-Eye a picture of say, a black pug, and this will be presented into the Third-Eye of their medium as such.

NOTES

It then depends on the medium's knowledge of the breeds of dog, plus its color, that will give to their consciousness the words "a black pug." Clairvoyance is invariably a combination of picture of faces, people, way of dress, along with objects with a flow of thought, giving names and other thought directives that follow on each other in a continuous flow. As a medium becomes more easily accustomed to receiving clairvoyance of an intuitive character, as has been described, so it may well be on special occasions, he will also receive objective clairvoyance too. Never try to seek in advance the type of clairvoyance one wishes to get, let it come and develop naturally. It is simply the imposing by your spirit guides or person of pictures and thought into your Third-Eye, in an attuned condition. No medium can create it their self, for if this is encouraged it will be your medium's imagination that will take place of the real thing, and they will only obstruct their development.

CLAIRSENTIENCE

Clairsentience is your inner sense of knowing (empathy); we are able feel another's illnesses, aches, pains, and all ranges of emotions within another person. It is also the vibes within a room as you walk in. Whether it is a party or an argument that just took place, it is your gut feeling from your solar plexus.

CLAIRAUDIENCE

Clairaudience is the hearing of spirit voices. Its effect can be very real, just as if someone's voice is being orally heard. In this respect, it can be linked to objective clairvoyance. For the simple reason that the words heard are not audible to another, or to any sound recording device, they do not exist physically at all. The physical ears do not receive it. The explanation is, that it is the spirit ear of their medium's spirit body that receives these spirit sound radiations which are transmitted in the Third-Eye, where they are interpreted into the form of words that your mind can appreciate, in the same way that he hears physical sounds.

NOTES

Like objective clairvoyance, this is a rare form of mediumship. Intuitive clairaudience is the more general rule when these impressions come; it is as if a medium is listening to thoughts which form noiselessly in their ears (a form of telepathy). This is the way it is sensed. Another way that the consciousness receives thought impressions is in the form of words. In public mediumship, we may see a medium appear as if they are listening with their ears. While there is no real harm in this, it is apparent to knowledgeable observers that they cannot receive physical audible words from spirit in their ears. This appearance of physically listening is but a way of inviting communication by adopting the act of listening. A student is advised to avoid this simulation, for no words are audibly heard, whether objective or intuitive. It is helpful when seeking any form of mental mediumship to close your eyes, especially when sitting for development. If your eyes are open, they cannot help but register in your Third-Eye that which they are seeing, in the beginning it is best to keep this as clear as possible. As your mediumship advances, your normal vision becomes just a background to your consciousness (just like music can be, while one is actively engaged in reading). Your open eyes enable a medium to observe their recipient of the message. This has its good and bad aspects, while a medium is able to observe their recipient's manner of their acceptance of the evidence provided, they can also see when it is not, and this can be disconcerting and tends to lead a medium into mental tenseness, and to stressfully seek explanations or escape routes. Intuitive clairaudience is a subtle condition. It can be described as listening-in to a soundless voice. As a rule, it is best to accept any such impression as coming from spirit and wait for confirmation. As a medium develops it will become very clear whether the words or message are spirit directed or not.

NOTES

There is no significance in either a blue or red light being used in a developing circle (the red light having a lower light frequency is thought to be the best) the only value is to give the students a sense of assurance, which may be absent in total darkness, and to prevent strong visual images being recorded in the consciousness.

TRANCE

The primary purpose that a majority of students seek in their development circle is "to go under control," and to receive their guides. It may be mentioned now, that trance states can vary from one percent to ninety-nine percent. The understanding of what does happen when your guides assume "control" will simplify your development, and will at the same time, discount a number romantic and fanciful ideas that are commonly current. For example, it is said that for a guide to "come in" a student's spirit mind and body must "go out." From this has arisen the notion that their guide's body enters within a mediums' physical body. We can understand how this idea has gained support, for when a student, whose mind is quick to act to suggestion, is told that they have a guide who is very big and broad (usually Zeus or a Red Indian) the thought is registered in a student's sub-conscious mind and hence as he feels their subtle mental change as the control becomes close, so he (probably is imitation what they have seen with others) induces a state of physical bigness by stretching their height and swelling out their chest. If they are told their guide is a Chinaman, they will let their shoulders slope down bending their head downwards, cross their hands over their chest in what is conceived to be a humble Chinese posture. If they are told they have an Indian guide they will use words like "moon for month, "wigwam" for house, "papoose" for child. Or if it is a Scottish guide they will speak in an induced Scottish dialect. At the risk of upsetting a medium, my opinion to these "characteristics" is unnecessary and rises from a student's inducement of them and it is very easy to fall into these errors.

NOTES

Such individual characteristics will not prevent a student developing trance control, indeed it may, subconsciously, aid it; the point is made that it is not factual or necessary. It is simply exhibitionism and posturing. True as it may be, that if your guide is a big fellow, a student will become conscious of this through their "nearness" of their guide's personality, and becomes receptive to the idea that their guide is taking physical possession of their body and so encouraging the characteristic. Here are a few examples I experienced to show how exaggerations can be built up upon wrong assumptions. At one developing circle, teachers told their students that as their guide "came in" so their spirit body went out, and was joined by a silver cord to a medium's body, and students were cautioned not to move for fear they became entangled with this cord. At another circle, students could not start until their teacher "heard" the clanking up the stairs of the metal-shod feet of St. George, and until this teacher could "see" him come through the door in full armor, before which he stood guard. When he drew his sword and held it at the "present" position it was safe for students to commence. Incidentally, at this circle we saw a man under alleged trance crawl round the floor on his knees, presenting each student a water lily. Next another man, who had a warrior guide, did a shadow sparring match before another student to bring the latter guide through forcibly. A little later on this same man adopted the pose of fishing, eventually went through the actions of landing a big fish. This was explained by a medium that this spirit person crossed over from lightning while fishing six hundreds years ago, and ever since he had been earth-bound trying to land the fish and now it that it was caught the spirit entity was free to go on his way. This circle ended with this medium being "entranced" by a noted female murderess, which had that morning been hanged. This is the sort of sheer nonsense I have observed in developing circles, and these illustrations are simply given to tell you as the reader that, should you ever be invited to attend a circle where such silliness prevails, you should bid the circle adieu.

NOTES

The pity of this was, in my opinion, that there were apparently a number of sincere students who accepted these happenings as being authentic. True it is that these events happened years ago, and it is hoped that they do not do so today, but we still hear from time to time of a strange "going-on." What happens in trance is simply this: The student's mental organization is taken over by the intelligence of their guide, and nothing more. The guide's body, being non-material and of spirit, cannot take over possession of a student's physical body. Their guide's control of their medium is purely mental. There is no physical incoming. When your guide takes over control of their medium's mental organization, they naturally control the body movement, use of arms and legs, as they take over the use of their vocal cords. They will also be aware of sound via their medium's ears and is able to answer questions. Consider an experience sometimes seen with trance mediumship, when speech is given in broken English. What happens is this, under a condition of trance control the guide conveys a thought flow through to their medium's consciousness where it is translated into words within their medium's knowledge. It is their medium's mind that translates the thought into pseudo Indian words. There is no need for a perverted dialect. Is it to be thought that an evolved guide, possessing great wisdom, has needed to talk in an ignorant and unlettered way? If other words come properly in English, why should the word "wigwam" be used for house, and the word "moon" to be used for month? If mediumship is to advance and be true, and a beginner is to take advantage of a more enlightened way of seeking their mediumship, they will avoid the unnecessary dress-up impersonation of dialect. Guides have a distinct personality and this is conveyed through their medium, in the same way that one can, to a lesser extent, be conscious of their personality as a friend.

NOTES

Therefore, it should be that a student will express under trance, the dignity and demeanor reflected through them, this can be different and almost too degrading in their mediumship that when they receive a broken English, accompanying a puffing out of their chest, a message alone is fine and yes, in trance your are fifty percent aware of your surroundings, so the puffing of the chest is mere EGO. One also hears the story that with the coming of the guide, they cannot speak because they know no English, and a period of time has to be allowed for them to learn it. This is but another "old-wives' tale" for, as has been shown, your guide does not need to learn words to be said; all they need to do is to convey their thoughts to their medium's mind to translate them into words. For the reason that contact is established by your guides through your mental process, there is no reason to suggest that your guides must be physically near their medium. They are able to tune-in from afar, even though a student senses their "nearness," which is a matter of appreciation. Sensing of your guide's presence is very real; it should not be denied or obstructed. They should be welcomed and acknowledged by a student, and as your affinity strengthens, so will students attuned mind which will become extra alert and sensitive. Breathing may quicken, your rhythm becomes faster, this should not be checked, and before long it will smooth out again as your guides announce their presence. The reason for this is not necessarily an occult one. When, in normal life, we anticipate an unusual event, we find the heart accelerates and your breathing will quicken, it may be that it is your subconscious anticipating the coming of your guides that induce this. With experience, and you becoming accustomed to contacting their guides, you will see that this acceleration in breathing will die away, and is a sign of a "developed medium." Quickened respirations may also present a mental expectation for your guide to take control, psychologically preparing their medium for this. Back in the day, quickened breathing rhythm should be allowed to carry on, until it eases down again.

NOTES

If, however, it becomes stressful, your circle teacher should check this in a nice way. As your guides obtain control of your mental equipment, there may also be a desire to stand up, to speak. This is unnecessary, for your guides will use your mind just as easily with you sitting in a restful way. Any tendency for a developing medium to stand and walk about in the circle should be checked, for this leads to silly extravagances, such as admiring "pretty beads," or a "pretty blouse." On the other hand, a medium can assist their guides by co-operating in a reasoned and common-sense way. For example, in the old days, a student was encouraged to assist their faculties to respond to impressions. If you have the desire to speak words, then you should assist to willingly voice them. A student may feel their throat constricted when first control is experienced, and words need to be said, but finds they cannot get out these words. When this happens, a student subconsciously should make the effort to encourage their voice to respond. Once this has been achieved it will come progressively easier in the future. Invariably, a student's eyes will be closed, almost unable to open them, and should not try to, unless they desire to return to normal. A good reason for this is, if your eyes were open they could not help but register what they see in their Third-Eye, this would, back in the day, interfere with its occupation by their guides. When a guide uses their medium's voice and mind it will appear to a student as if they are listening to their self speaking these words. The thought flow will come uninterrupted, without any need for a medium to "think" what is coming next. He will know very well when thought flow has ended, and then they will be ready to prepare to return to normal and regain their self. While your guide is speaking, you should enjoy it, never interfering with it in any way. If you do you will find it will cease, and cannot carry on. You may even be conscious of a wrong word used or mispronounced as a re-correction naturally comes, if it does not, show or make no effort to interfere with the flow of words. Their speech may convey a different characteristic to that of their medium's normal speech.

NOTES

It may be more authorative, possessing dignity, this is to be expected, for your guide's personality will be expressed not yours. A medium should not alter this; add to it, for it leads to exhibitionism. They may still desire their consciousness to become blank to reassure them self, but this cannot be. They will, however, realize that the flow of words come from them in speech, and are not of their conscious creation. There will be new thoughts, constructions, and new phrases that are used that they do not know meaning to, and at the risk of repetition, the reason for this is that it is their mental equipment that is being subconsciously used to dress their guide's thoughts in words that are limited to their vocabulary. Evidence of this is seen when a poorly developed medium with a Red Indian guide, will only use words such as, "moon, " "papoose," "wigwam" and "Squaw," because they are only Indian words they know. You may read of mediums speaking in intelligent foreign tongues of which a medium has no knowledge, sometimes of a remote language. This is a phrase of advanced or unusual mediumship that is above this study. It is often associated with "physical mediumship." Speaking in distinct Chinese or Sanskrit evolves an entirely different process. This is far different from the nonsense jargon I have heard some through some mediums, for this is often nothing more than nonsense. Every good circle teacher will stop this, with the instruction that if their guide is truly in possession of a medium's mind, they will use it properly. When trance speaking comes, it may be that a medium is conscious of their arms and hands moving to give force and emphasis to their message. This is a natural flow of your mind acting to express intention of words by action. It may be guide directed, it may be your subconscious use of the arms by a medium's mind. This should not be interfered with, unless there is undue exaggeration by reason of subconscious excitement.

NOTES

If this takes place, a medium should be given the directive for more orderly conduct in the future. Sometimes, back in the olden days of development, excessive and unreasonable actions and behaviors were seen. It is your duty as a teacher of the circle to correct this, and the student should seek more orderly control. Mediumship should be dignified and natural, even developing mediums should seek to attain this. It may be their guides in their willingness to use their human instrument more condone weaknesses, such as the use of broken English, to interfere, for the unnecessary practices are the product of a medium's mind and not your guides. This brings us to another important consideration in development, transfiguration.

NOTES

TRANSFIGURATION

As your guides take over your direction of your mind and a state of control draws near, your breathing rhythm will become accelerated, this should be allowed to continue, your face may feel as if changes are taking place. This gives rise to the idea, especially in red light, that a student is being transfigured by their guide (over shadowed) when most times it is nothing of the sort. The gift of transfiguration is a rare one. It is usually associated with physical mediumship; a true transfiguration needs to be formed over an ectoplasmic base. While it may be reassuring, and appeals to the romantic side, if a beginner is told they are being transfigured by their guide, well then, it is better to avoid this delusion, or misguided by the sincere imagination of others present in the circle. While the teacher of the circle will be able to clairvoyantly "see" the guide with the student, this is not necessarily transfiguration. Simulation of transfiguration by students or even some mediums, especially if they have mobile faces, can easily be induced in dim or red lights, and a sincere student should not be persuaded by the comment of others, proven transfiguration mediums are very rear. Physical mediumship is an advanced state of mediumship possessing a higher spiritual order.

NOTES

AUTOMATIC WRITING

Automatic writing is linked to trance speech, the difference being the hand is used to transcribe the intuitive thought flow instead of speaking it. Do not, however, expect the hand to suddenly proceed to write, as some beginners are told to expect, this is unlikely. You will be conscious, within you mind, of the formation of thought that you watch your hand write, as in trance speech. Mediums do not find it necessary to create their written thoughts themselves, but to just allow the thought intentions to flow, and the hand to write them down. Your hand is often unable to write quickly enough to keep up with it, so writing degenerates into scribble. If automatic writing is to be encouraged, then there should be imposed a degree of self-discipline to keep writing orderly. As a rule, those who have no personal desire to speak in public under trance, find that automatic writing is a way in which to allow their guides to express themselves through their medium. There are always those who possess particular gifts of the spirit to a degree, and this applies to all forms of mediumship. With automatic writing, we have the very exceptional spirit-inspired Scripts from all over the world, from Moses to Nostradamus. Writing should be personal benefit, instruction and advancement of a medium; some received writings should be discouraged for publication. It is natural that a medium who is able to write inspirationally, is very proud, but often the themes of writing is of theological character, pointing out the way of right living, and the medium desires that other may profit from their teachings. But in fact, there have been thousands of manuscripts written that have been submitted to publishers, but very few have been seen their way into print and only then at the medium's expense. However, if a beginner has an inner desire to let their hand act as a transcriber of spirit thought, they can do so. They should wait for a quiet time, so their outlook is contented and they are ready to enter attunement with their guides. They should have a pen and a pad of paper available.

NOTES

As they feel the influence of their guides draw within their aura their thoughts are taken over, he should write them down. Just as in trance speech when a medium listens to them self speak, so in writing they are as "an observer," to watch their hand write words and phrases. Once your hand becomes the agent for the thought flow, it should not be interfered with in any way, nor should the writing be questioned, or the words to come be anticipated. With usage, your guide will regulate the thought flow to the speed that your hands can write legibly. Many specimens of automatic writing you see are lines of almost unintelligible scribble with one word running into another. This is untidy and poor mediumship. In trance speech the voice may carry an effect of a different personality, so it may be in writing the character of this may vary from a medium's usual calligraphy. In trance speech your eyes are closed, but in writing they are open as observers of what is taking place. In automatic writing, there is a greater chance of a medium's mind superimposing itself over their guide's thought flow than in the case of trance speaking when the whole being is more tensed, but experience will overcome this. A medium should set their self a limit of time before they commence, say thirty minutes, this should not b exceeded. They should also sit for writing at definite time, or times in a week. Once is best, but twice should not be exceeded. Naturally, a student in their enthusiasm wishes to do as much as he can, and it may be their guide is anxious too, yet there is more need for self-discipline in writing than with other forms of mediumship, for it can tend to get out of hand, and this must be avoided at all costs, not only for the medium's peace of mind but for the sake of mediumship too.

~~~~~~~~NOTES~~~~~~~~

TABLE COMMUNICATION

There are various methods of table communication, such as the Ouija Board; using a glass to travel letters of the alphabet; table tipping, etc. A beginner is strongly advised to completely shun these methods and have nothing to do with them. So called "communications" obtained this way are most unreliable, but there have been exceptional instances, but as a general rules they are either the product from influencing (perhaps sub-conscious) on the part of someone present, or the sport of some undesirable mischievous spirit that is elemental and crude. It is from this undesirable practice that harm has come to those who indulge it, and reflect discredit on the good name of spirit. Have nothing to do with it at any time. Unless you are using the highest good for all!

MEDIUMSHIP CONCLUSION

It is desired; through this guide it will be observed; the development of spirit gifts is a natural process. A beginner should never accept anything that is said or written before their common-sense and to consider whether any act or statement is reasonable, and is supported by psychic science. The gift of mediumship must prove itself. It is a natural gift and therefore development is to follow out the natural processes. Just remember to ask your angels and guides for help with these five steps:

- Consistency
- Meditation
- Contemplation
- Intention
- Action

NOTES

"DO'S" AND "DON'TS"

- *Remember your guide is using your mind.*
- *Guides do not enter into physical possession of you body.*
- *Everything is mental appreciation, so is mediumship.*
- *Development means attunement.*
- *You cannot make your mind a blank.*
- *Mediumship is employment of your mind by your guide.*
- *Your consciousness interprets thoughts into words.*
- *Spirit vision is projections of pictures in your Third-Eye.*
- *You cannot reach attunement by concentration.*
- *Avoid imitating what others do, even mediums.*
- *Avoid exhibitionism, posturing, pigeon English and "baby-talk."*
- *Do not exaggerate clairvoyance.*
- *Do not interfere with a flow of thought from your guide.*
- *Have confidence in your guide.*
- *Follow the advice of your circle teacher.*
- *Maintain harmony in your developing circle.*
- *Do not listen to gossip about others in your circle.*
- *Maintain self-discipline.*
- *Never allow impressions of control to continue outside your developing circle.*
- *Always return to full normality before leaving the circle.*
- *Be master of your mediumship; do not let it master you.*

NOTES

- *Do not allow your guide to come close, unless invited to do so.*
- *Do not hold negative thoughts about your mediumship.*
- *Have patience, a slow development is generally best.*
- *Anticipate with pleasure your circle sittings.*
- *Always be punctual and regular in attendance.*
- *Have confidence that no harm can come to you.*
- *Always start your sitting with a prayer for guidance and protection.*
- *Enjoy being aware of your mediumship.*
- *The Other side is everywhere, it's all around us! It's pure energy, at a higher vibratory rate unseen y the human eye. There is only a mere thin layer of atmosphere between us and the Other Side. The only thing that separates us is a vibratory frequency.*
- *Everyone is born with a degree of psychic ability. It is how often we use it and how it becomes more apparent to ourselves.*
- *It doesn't matter what your religion is when you cross over because there is no type of religion on the Other Side. It is of pure love, faith, peace and harmony and only one Supreme Spirit so there is no need of any religious conflict.*
- *You are the mother of your own soul. Your soul needs unconditional love from you. It needs to be taught, nurtured and corrected just as you would with a child.*
- *Like attracts like or birds of a feather flock together. If you work for the highest good you will not attract bad or evil spirits to yourself nor will they affect you.*

NOTES

- *Different levels on the Other Side are determined by lessons and deeds accomplished while on the earth plane. This will happen immediately when you pass to spirit. You will gravitate to the proper level according to the compassion, kindness, assistance and unconditional love you displayed with others.*
- *Deceased spirit comes back to the earth plane to assist their loved ones in trying times or for upliftment. Mostly they come back for special occasions such as weddings, births, deaths, anniversaries, and birthdays.*
- *People do not change in appearance when they cross over because they like to be recognized by loved ones seeking them so they show themselves as they were before they passed over*
- *All your earthly functions are done by thought or telepathy, so don't worry if you have deceased ancestors of a different language, communication is done by thought.*
- *Suicide victims do show themselves the same way any deceased love one does. They always show remorse for what they did and say frequently; even when you die you can't run from your problems because there is no death therefore there is no escape from your dilemmas. When they come through, send them enormous amount of healing to assist them in their healing process.*
- *Mediums do not call 1-888-MIA-SOUL; we do not call up the dead. They have free will as they did on the earth plane. Mediums cannot guarantee who will come through.*
- *Reincarnation has been proven through De`ja`vue and past life regressions. We are reincarnated approximately every 100 to 200 years according to the person's free will if they want to return sooner or not return at all.*

NOTES

- *Cultivate a high code of spiritual values in daily life.*
- *Avoid meanness of thought, be generous in all things.*
- *When control approaches, encourage it by making efforts to speak, etc.*
- *In description, describe only what you see, and not what you think.*
- *Never interpose your own thoughts over those of your guide.*
- *In sitting, be comfortable, loosen tight clothing.*
- *In sitting, put all thoughts of mundane matters out of mind, be happy within.*
- *Know your guide is always with you.*
- *Cultivate an inwardly contented outlook day by day, and enjoy life.*
- *Do not make yourself artificial or think you are super spiritual.*
- *Be natural, enjoy humor, and look for happiness in all things.*

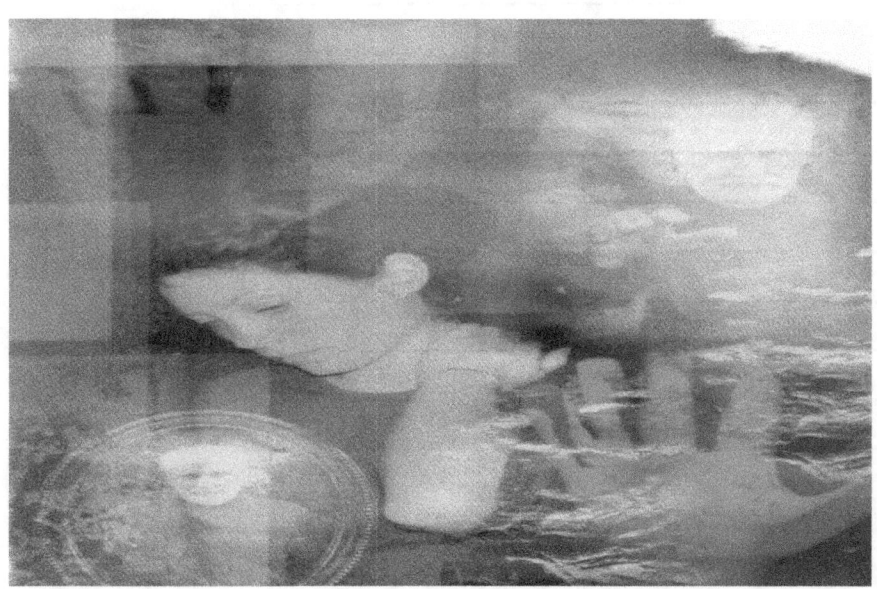

NOTES

CHAPTER VIII

KUNDALINI

Your Kundalini is a serpent of pure energy that lies asleep at the base of the spine, coiled 31/2 times around the first chakra waiting for enfoldment. When it is awakened, it unfolds and rises through the center of the body piercing and awakening each chakra as it climbs upward. When it rises to the top to your crown chakra, then all your chakras have been opened causing enlightenment. Usually the feeling is a rush or a chill going up and down the spine.

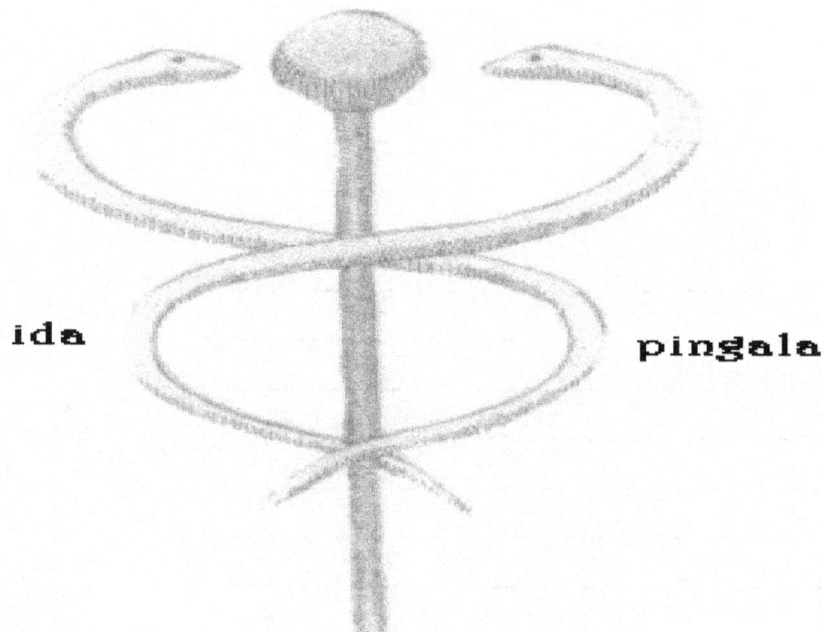

Kundalini Force. "Serpent Fire."

NOTES

THE CHAKRAS

Chakras means "wheel" in Sanskrit (a classical Old Indic Literary language, as cultivated from the 4th century B.C. onward and still used in the ritual of the Northern Buddhist Church: because of the antiquity of its written expression and the detail descriptive analysis in the Sutras. Sanskrit has been very important in the origin and development of comparative Indo- European Root Race linguistics. Sutras means: Buddha dialogue) this wheel are the chakras and the centers where energy can flow into the body. Their size, color and brilliance may vary according to an individual's state of health and development. They appear as vortexes on the energy body or etheric double, the field of life-force which emanates or vitalizes the dense physical body. Beyond etheric double is the glow of your aura, by reading auras, you may learn a lot about yourself or others.

- *Sahasrara Crown or coronal chakra, on the top of the head. Rules higher knowledge.*
- *Ajna Third-eye or brow, frontal chakra, between eyebrows. Rules intuitive psyche.*
- *Vishuddah Throat or laryngeal chakra, front throat. Rules communications.*
- *Anahata Heart or cardiac chakra, just over the heart. Rules Unconditional Love.*
- *Manipuri A. Solar Plexus or over the navel, umbilical chakra. Rules vital energies.*
- *Manipura B. Spleen or splenic chakra. Used by some authorities as sexual chakra.*
- *Svadhishthana Sexual at the ovaries or testicles. Rules desires and passion.*
- *Muladhara Root or base chakra at the base of the spine. Rules survival*
- *Hand chakras, considered minor, in palms toward the web of thumb. Rules action.*
- *Foot chakras, minor, middle of arches. Rules grounding and independence.*

An energy channel called Sushumna runs up through the central chakras, intertwining through it and the chakras. These energy channels are "feminine (left side)" and "masculine (right side)" channels, called the Ida and the pingala. Through these may flow the "Serpent Fire" or the Kundalini Force. Awakening and controlling this power is a goal for anyone trying to reach enlightenment.

NOTES

Seven Major chakras run the center of your body, however, there are many throughout the body.

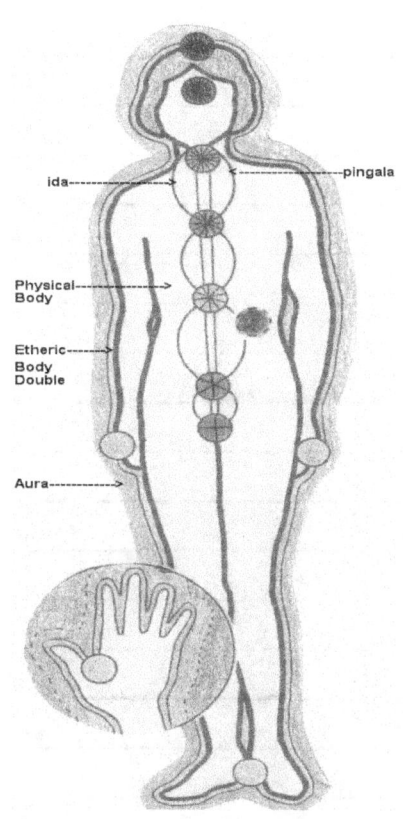

NOTES

SEVEN EYES

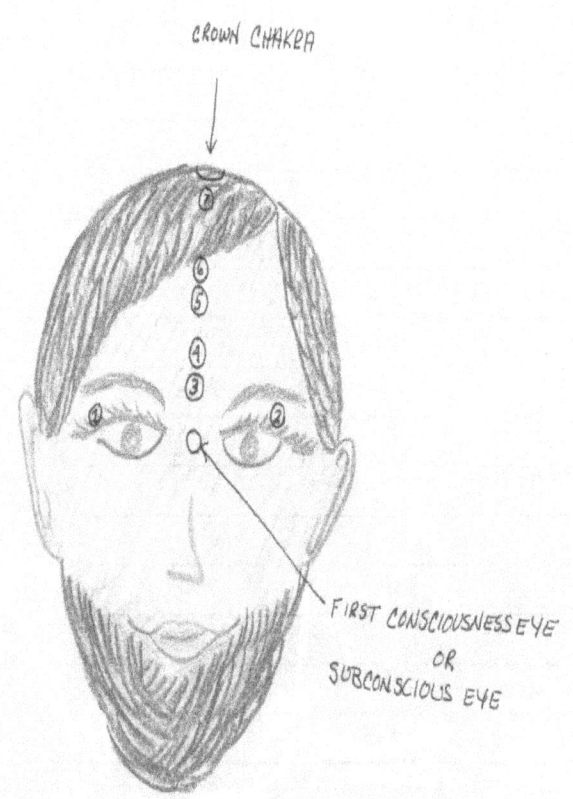

NOTES

In addition to your physical two eyes, there are five additional spiritual eyes that form your expanded awareness.

- *The first is your right eye that is used to see forms of objects in perception to details.*
- *The second is your left eye used in analyzing emotions and colors and is more perceptive to texture than to form. It also senses relationships between objects.*
- *The third eye enlarges what the first two eyes sees and brings depth and/or a third dimension. Located between the eyebrows.*
- *The fourth eye understands relationships and developing a belief in the divine. It enlarges what the other eyes see. Located just above the third eye.*
- *The fifth eye aids in understanding universal truths and ideals; with it we receive "concepts" and it is excellent for past life viewing. Located in the center of the forehead*
- *The sixth eye is necessary for true inner sight and for understanding the essence and purpose of our lives. Located just below the hair line.*
- *The seventh eye aids in understanding the totality and purpose of the universe; through it we receive divine understanding and see radiant light and angelic presences. Located about an inch above the hair line.*
- *The second first consciousness eye or the subconscious eye is located at the top of the nose, at the indentation below the bones that rise up to form the brow. It is an area of combined physical and emotional consciousness and as such relates to your basic or primitive living, gut feelings, basic survival and awareness. With this chakra opened, it puts a person in touch with the subconscious (which is not supposed to be subconscious at all.) Any emotional or physical difficulties that a person chooses not to deal with on a conscious level will produce blocks, inhibiting growth and awareness. When it is too opened it is in reversal and you are too preoccupied becoming out of touch with your true self. Few people have all seven eyes developed; few in fact, have even the first two eyes developed. This is mainly due to ignorance of the possibilities in the various forms of sight, our own laziness in comprehending or "seeing" what our eyes actually view, and insufficient regard for our spiritual heritage of expanded consciousness. All of these attitudes put veils over our eyes; but when remove the veils a whole new world opens up.*

NOTES

COLOR HEALING

Light is radiant energy traveling in the forms of waves. The rate of vibration can be measured in units known as the Angstrom units (one hundred – millionth of a centimeter, a unit used in measuring the length of light waves), each color is measured by 1/10 millionth of a millimeter. Your body selects from the sunlight, whatever colors are needed for balance, the vibrations are then absorbed into you. The technique of healing with color is to give the ill body an extra dose of colors the body is lacking. This is one of the joyful ways to do a healing because it is harmless and we only use natural elements. This technique can be done numerous ways. Basically, the red end of the spectrum stimulates while the blue end calms. You don't have to be in the sunlight to do this. Have the person sit facing frontward in front of a window and tape the appropriate see through stone to the affected area of the body, I recommend glass-like stones not agates, which are very solid, the sun would not penetrate through them and reach the affected area. Example: for an upset stomach, direct yellow light on the stomach area. Concentrate the light on that area for at least thirty minutes each time. You can do distant healing as well, by using either a photograph or just imaging them with their ailment and project the color to them where needed. When using the photograph, place the appropriate stone in the area of ailment for the same amount of time, thirty minutes, and everyday until ailment subsides. Included are the specific colors of the spectrum and their healing properties:

NOTES

- *Red is a warm invigorating color used for treating blood diseases, anemia, liver infections, or just grounding and success.* Use red garnet or rubies. The antidote is aquamarine or light blue topaz.
- *Orange is not quite as strong as red, yet it contains many of the properties of red and is used for the respiratory system, asthma, bronchitis, a laxative, or to relieve shyness and the sense of resentment, use* carnelian. *The antidote is blue sapphire.*
- *Yellow is used for the bowels and intestines. It is a mild laxative and sedative for removal of fears and a mental upliftment. It is also used for indigestion, heartburn, constipation, piles, and yes, menstrual problems. It also re-establishes your will power to conquer any defeat or obstacles in your way, use* citrine. *As an antidote use* amethyst.
- *Green is the color of great healing and is neutral for other colors because it is a revitalizer. When in doubt, use* green. *Green is used for heart trouble, neuralgic, headaches, ulcers, head colds, and boils. Green is used also to bring more love and compassion into the heart.* Use emerald, *because this is a neutral color, no antidote is necessary, since it is central and balanced.*
- *Blue is used as an antiseptic and a cooling agent for cuts, burns, rheumatism, or any inflammations of the internal organs and to help you speak freely with love.* Use aquamarine or light blue topaz. *As an antidote use* tigers-eye.
- *Indigo is slightly narcotic and will remove fears of the mind and reassurances. Indigo is a great color for emotional disorders, deafness, especially great for eyes, or cataracts, also used to open your third-eye and mentally see clearly.* Use Lapis Lazuli, *as an antidote use* carnelian.
- *Violet is great for mental disorders, the nervous system, and balding. It is also used to access the unconscious and subconscious.* Use sugulite, *and as an antidote use* citrine.

Antidotes are used if you feel over or under aggressive in a particular section of your chakras.

NOTES

OPEN THE HAND CHAKRAS TO HEAL

Sit comfortably with your hands pushed straight out in front of you, elbows straight. Turn one palm upward and one downward. Quickly, with repeated motions, open and close fists tightly, as fast and as long as you comfortably can. Switch positions of your palms and repeat until your hands are tired. Drop your arms, open your fists and bring your palms together slowly, moving them together and out again. Do you feel a ball of energy between your hands? If you tune in closely, you can actually feel the spinning.

HEALING

There are two forms of healing. The first is lying of the hands and the second is distant healing, where the individual needs not be present to be healed. Healing is now considered, by many, the highest form of mediumship. Perhaps this gift of healing must possess a high spiritual quality. Whereas the development of purely psychic faculties needs to possess a spiritual incentive, healing certainly does. The primary qualities a healer possesses are those of generosity, love, and a yearning to heal the sick, and to take away any distress. Spiritual healing is a spirit science; while this is true of all forms of mediumship, healing by the nature of its accomplishments needs the presence of your guide or guides, who have the particular knowledge how to direct the correct qualitative remedial forces to master a given ill condition. It is very true that every guide possesses knowledge of this character to some degree, but it is reasonable to assume that as the healing gift develops it will become necessary for other spirit personalities to come into the picture for dealing with specific diseases. The gift of healing is an involved process. The commencement of healing mediumship invariably begins in a healing circle, particularly so, when you as a student is able to receive a condition of trance. Many healers have commenced their ministry under trance, and then as the development precedes the need for a trance state is overcome. This follows the acceptance of the fact that their guides are always present when there is a need for their services, and they are able to direct the healing forces to the patient via the healer's spirit faculties without trance being essential. It is suggested that a beginner who desires to develop healing, should when they have been able to attain attunement, attend a healing circle, first as an observer, and then, later on, to join in with the healing endeavor through their spirit self, as if he is actually taking part in the healing itself. Absent Healing is usually done within a healing circle or a healing service by just sending their name into the ether and wish them healing. This can be done even with a person who severely induced with negativity, illnesses, incarcerated mentally or physically in need of being uplifted. It is taking the power of your intentions, raising your power and directing toward the person who is ill. <u>Under no circumstances should you ever advise a person not to follow their doctor's advice or to not seek the aid of a professional therapist. And never prescribe anything; always have them refer to their physician.</u>

NOTES

THE AURA

The aura consists of metabolism that operates in two ways, first being the Katabolic force breaks down complex chemical compounds of our body into a simple form which are expelled from the body. The second is the anabolic forces builds up from simple compounds supplied by your food and drink the highly complex compounds which replace those already broken down and eliminated. There is a cycle of breaking down and building up in constant progress. Varying rates and ratios of this metabolic process result in various conditions of the physical body, it is one of the teachings that the metabolic process are initiated from and controlled by the body of finer pre-matter which is the etheric body. This finer body has many names, the Egyptians of old called it "Ka," in Medieval Europe, they called it "Doppelganger," in the Middle East, they called "Lingo Shari rah," In France, they called it "Per sprit," and we call it the astral body or the aura. There are three levels to the aura. The first is the physical body. The second is the etheric body that protects and maintains the physical body. The third is your spiritual aura that extends beyond the etheric aura by a few feet to many yards according to how evolved spiritually you are.

HOW TO VIEW THE AURA

Stand the subject eighteen inches in front of a plain white background. Have the person relax and breathe deeply. For best viewing, you need to be at least ten feet away, and the lights should not be too bright or focused directly on the subject. Natural lighting is best. The technique to view the aura requires that you look past the head and shoulder area. Focus on the wall behind the figure. As you stare past the outline of the body, you will very quickly notice a fuzzy white or grayish silver envelope surrounding the body. It almost looks like a light is behind the person, pointing up. Then most probably it will disappear. That is because the natural reaction of most people as they first see this envelope is to inadvertently change their focus to the person and not continue to stare at the wall. As soon as you go back focusing on the background, the envelope will reappear. You must train your eye not to revert to normal focus-that is the hardest thing to learn. Once you have mastered maintaining your gaze through the person, you will notice that colors, shapes, rays and even secondary auric fields will be readily visible.

NOTES

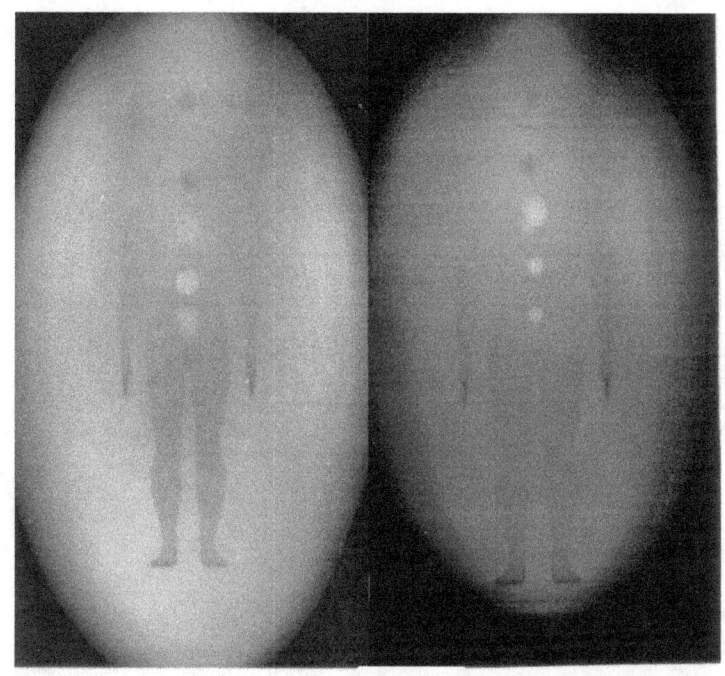

JEFF

3/13/07 3:56 PM

JEFF

3/13/07 4:01 PM

This is my husband Jeffery's aura taken this past month. As you can see the aura extends considerably and his chakras are all well aligned. This is of an average individual, who is well balanced, and enjoys life. As you can see they change considerably just within five minutes. His aura was larger and his chakras changed as well. In the left illustration he had just came in from a walk, the second illustration, he was sitting for just a few minutes and is more relaxed and speaking from the heart, see how his heart chakra has grown. The first illustration shows a more playful color of aqua green while the second illustration show a more spiritual color of cyan blue.

NOTES

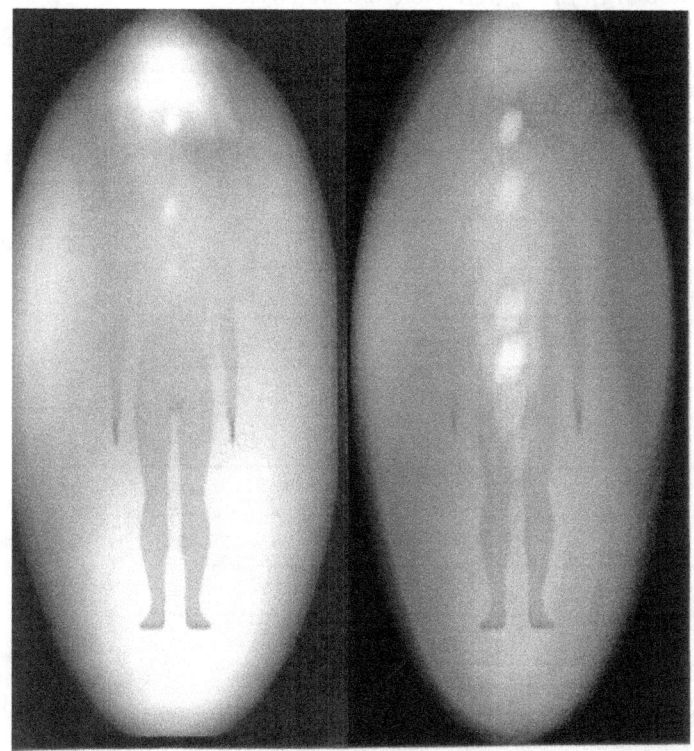

These are mine on the same date as my husbands. The illustration to the left is at the beginning of my day at work. The illustration to your right is after I've done psychic reading for the day. Notice how stressed the chakras are and how the color has changed from crystal to cyan blue in the right illustration, this is called channeled, notice how my heart chakra disappeared; speaking from the heart. The illustration to the left is my norm, chakras all aligned and same forms. And the crown is wide open ready to read. This color of crystal and lavender and type of aura is usually considered an aura of a blue ray child, or of the new indigo, crystal, or rainbow children sent to us today.

NOTES

SOUL MATES/TWINFLAMES

Relationships are mirrors that help us learn more about ourselves. They are the most challenging and the most rewarding aspects of life. The more intimate the relationship the greater the opportunity for growth we are given. There are three different types of relationship mirrors. One is the mirror of who you were. This mirror gives you the opportunity to see how far you have come, the chance to experience karma that you have already cleared. So don't get caught up in this relationship worried about why it is coming back at this time, thank it and let it go. The second type of relationship is the one that is mirroring where you are now on your path. If an issue or person has an emotional "charge" to it, then you still have work to do. This mirror is the hardest to look through because it reflects the issues you have not yet finished in your life. These are the things that we are the most blind to. The last type of relationship is the one that mirrors your potential. This allows you to have a glimpse at who you could be, if you wanted to. This person is usually someone that you idealize and put on a pedestal or look up to. Take a look at your various relationships and see which group they fall into. By knowing this you will gain insight into yourself. Self understanding is the entire reason for these mirrors, not to "fix" the other person, but to look at yourself and learn. The primary reason for most relationships is so you can work on your spiritual self and your karma! So with that said, the more you clear up issues for yourself, the more you ARE the "right" person; the more you will attract the person you are looking for. As you continue to work on yourself you will meet many potential partners, in every facet of life. From the point of view of Love relationships, though you may meet someone and the connection was so strong that it almost takes your breath away. You may have the experience of knowing someone's thoughts and feelings, almost before they do. When this happens you probably have connected with someone who is your Soul Mate or perhaps even your Twin Flame. So now, What s a Soul Mate? Soul Mates are those beings that we have had connections with in past lives. They may have been our parents, siblings, spouses, friends, etc. and they have agreed to come back to join us again. The reason for this rejoining is so that we can each achieve balance in our lives. Our Soul Mates represent our spiritual family. By connecting with them we are reminded of the resonance of our Soul and also they help us to wake up and remember our purpose. Most of the time when we think of Soul Mates we are thinking of love relationships, but we can have Soul Mates that join us for business partnerships, healing relationships, and yes, love relationships. Any relationship we can have is open arena of Soul Mates. They may be a teacher or minister or counselor who comes into our life and touches it deeply. Soul Mates are truly our friends from many lifetimes who come to play again with us on this earth. Often they come into our lives for a specific time or event. They may even come into a love relationship to assist us in a specific learning event and then move on. Whatever the purpose is of being in each others lives it is a beautiful experience.

NOTES

When you connect with your Soul Mate in a love relationship, you have, in effect, found your perfect mate for where you are in your development as a Soul. So if Soul Mates are our spiritual family, what are Twin Flames? Twin Flames are ourselves in another body. When Souls chose to enter into physicality, they were split into masculine and feminine aspects. Please note, I did not say male and female, because throughout our incarnations, we will be in both genders of bodies. When we first leave the Light to enter into physicality, we will connect with our Twin Flame. This is done so we will not feel so totally alone in the human experience. After this we go our separate ways and grow lifetime after lifetime in experience and wisdom until we are ready to break free of the bonds of physicality and mortality. When we have reached this stage, we have the opportunity to reconnect with our "other half" or Twin Flame.

The chances are that we meet our Twin Flame briefly in many lifetimes, but one or both of us are not ready for the intensity of this connection. When both halves of the whole are ready to come back together and meet they will discover that in that lifetime they have lead almost parallel lives. The events of their lives will mirror each other almost exactly. They may have come from very similar families and family dynamics. They have had similar schooling or lack thereof. They may have almost identical careers. They may even have previous marriages and divorces within weeks of each other; they will feel as if the other is reading their life script. Once in a relationship, the bond between Twin Flames can only be compared to the bond between identical twins. They are aware of each others thoughts, feelings, desires and needs at a level that is hard to imagine. The depth of Love is such that to be apart even for a day is a hardship. What is meant by that is that their hearts literally hurt when they are separated from each other, even if it is only for the work day. It is this depth of Love that reminds them of the Oneness of Light to which they are returning. By anchoring this Love in the physical, not only are they preparing for their own ascension, but they are also leaving an imprint for others to follow in time for their own. All relationships serve a purpose and should be honored and appreciated for what they have to offer you in your personal spiritual growth. Thank the person and the experiences for all that you have had the opportunity to learn and clear. Know that ALL relationships are sacred, because they bring us closer to the Light of All That Is.

NOTES

NOTES

PRECIOUS STONES

- Amber……………………....protection, cleansing, calming, infections, absorbs and transmutes negative energy.
- Amethyst…………………..spiritual awareness, dreaming, dispels nightmares, protection, known as the helps eliminate O.C.D.
- Aquamarine……………….builds up courage.
- Aventurine………………...good luck, abundance, adventures in travel, healing the heart, emotions, and self-love.
- Axinite……………………...attracts new friendships.
- Black tourmaline………….deflects negativity, calms, grounding, reduces anger, protection shield eases obsessions.
- Bloodstone………………...childbirth, stops bleeding, inflammations, balances emotions, grounding and protection.
- Carnelian…………………..reproduction, sexuality, menstrual cramps, lungs, creative visualization, stimulate emotions, arthritis.
- Citrine……………………...self-esteem, joy, clears thinking, merchants' stone.
- Clear Quartz……………....transmitter and transducer that aids in thought and energy. Amplifies thoughts and intentions, activates focused positive energy
- Copper……………………..arthritis, stimulates optimism, good luck.
- Emerald…………………....successful love, domestic bliss, stimulates heart, chakra, harmony, fidelity, joy, all healing.
- Garnet……………………...sexuality, taking action, commitment, stimulate the kundalini, energy.
- Hematite…………………....calming, high blood pressure, transforms negativity, muscle cramps, nervous disorders, insomnia, grounding.
- Jade………………………...fidelity, dreamtime, harmony, wisdom, protection, good luck, abundance, heart, tranquility
- Jasper……………………...supreme nurturer, grounding, facilitates safe astral travel, protection.
- Lapis lazuli………………...total awareness, activates throat, third-eye, and crown chakras, emotional balance, PMS, protection, insomnia, dreaming, woman's healing, depression, infections.

NOTES

- Leopard Skin Agate……….assists in strength and endurance.
- Malachite…………………..clears emotional blocks, eyesight, absorbs negativity, digestion, diabetes, hypoglycemia, fidelity.
- Moonstone……………….....balancing, connect with feelings, emotional tension, travelers' stone, PMS, menopause, insomnia, dreams.
- Moss Agate…………………commands and promotes personal growth.
- Onyx………………………..happiness, repels negativity and bad feelings.
- Phantom Quartz……………universal awareness, past lives, emotional Healing.
- Pyrite………………………..grounding, protection, enhances memory recall.
- Red Jasper………………….grounding and balances sexual desires.
- Rhondonite…………………stone of love, lost love, energizes heart chakra, grounding, calming, brotherhood, unconditional love, self confidence.
- Rose quartz………………....stone of gentle love, peace, calming, nurturing, balances emotions, heals emotional wounds.
- Smokey quartz……………...collects scattered energies, dissolves negativity, clears emotional blocks, protection, stone of cooperation.
- Snowflake Obsidian………..third eye vision, aids in confusion in your opponent.
- Sodalite……………………..stabilizes mental and emotional processes, PMS, cramps, clears old patterns, migraines and headaches, wisdom, metabolism, and self esteem.
- Tiger Eye……………………stability, assists in speaking freely and what is on your mind, courage to stand up for yourself.
- Unikite……………………...erases insecurities and anxieties.

NOTES

TIDBITS

LAY UPON THE EARTH

Spirit of the Universe:	Spirit of the unknown path awaits our footsteps. I ask for guidance to make things fruitful, healthy, clear-sighted, and gentle on my heart.
Spirit of the Air:	Allow me thought and knowledge; lead me in the pursuit of new visions, to work toward new goals.
Spirit of the Earth:	Bring me prosperity, abundance, and joy in my career.
Spirit of the Flame:	Induce me with vitality and guide me toward Personal strength and good health.
Spirit of the Water:	Fill me with the appropriate emotions and bring forth my deepest psyche. Teach me love, empathize, and understand myself and others. Be with me in sorrow, joy, in turmoil, and Peace.

MYSTICAL POWERS

Mystical power flows naturally, only when an individual opens his or her consciousness fully. Opening is not instantaneous, it takes time, personal motivation, and a lot of introspection to move one's consciousness in a direction that is free from the influences of classifications, judgment, and mental associations such as, gender, social roles, culture orientation, geographic location, and so on.

ONENESS CONNECTION

You do not have to open a channel to the Divine Source, to the universal mind, to the ascendants. We are already connected. We always have been, we always will be, but what is necessary is that we remove self-destruction beliefs and behaviors blocking your conscious awareness. Once these blocks are removed or melted away and transformed, you can then, make use of your birthright. And that is to know! Imperfection is of the EGO, perfection is of the SOUL! Some people are accused of having an EGO, and it is usually by another trying to do just as well in their accomplishments that are not focused on the Light aspects and their work does not work for them because of their extreme dark-side taking over. So they result to tactics of accusing, in reality it is merely a jealousy tactic. It is their jealousy not your EGO!!! They are just trying to lower you to their level. Don't listen, just smile and move higher like you supposed to do without being held back by other insecurities.

NOTES

EMPATHY
(CLAIRSENTIENCE)

The root of the word empathy is PATHOS- the Greek word for feeling. Sympathy means acknowledging the feelings of someone else as in "I sympathize with you." Empathy is a term for a deeper feeling. It means "I feel what you feel. I can put myself in your shoes." Sympathy results in kindness and sometimes pity. Empathy results in actually feeling the pain, or the joy, of the other person. You can see how the willingness to be flexible comes more easily when you can put yourself in the other person's shoes. Empathy is a key skill taught in negotiating. Every human has a deep need for his/her feelings to be recognized. If you know this you can help tremendously in a difficult negotiation by creating a climate for agreements. It is important to acknowledge both factual points, and the feelings of the other person in any situation. The feeling of empathy is much easier to come by when you care about the other person and take time to feel what they're feeling. The feeling of empathy for others, start at the same point: You cannot truly feel the pain or the joy or the emotion of another until and unless you're able to feel the same thing in yourself. Do you acknowledge your own pain? Can you feel your own joy? Real empathy lies in simply finding the same place within you that the other person is experiencing. You might not have exactly the same experience but you've known the sadness of loss or the anger of feeling cheated, or the sense of righteousness at injustice. Some of us don't take the time to feel our own feelings, so when someone else expresses a feeling, we don't have much to refer to. Men are being encouraged to express and share their feelings more these days, and not just soft, vulnerable feelings, but feelings of anger and frustrations as well. You might be concerned that expressing a caring approach toward another person will result in the other person manipulating you. This isn't about abdicating your own needs or point of view. It simply means that you're able to step into the shoes of another and acknowledge their feelings. Having that ability is an asset. You can always wear your own shoes, and you do most of the time.

NOTES

QUOTES FOR FRIENDS

- *Stay fired up about living your highest potential, because part of our moral imperative is to inspire and empower not only ourselves, but one another.*
- *Life is not a dress rehearsal and we're all in the same boat; no matter where you live or the color of your skin, if you breathe oxygen we are all on the same boat. Like it or not, if part of this boat sinks, we all sink.*
- *Every decision we make, large or small impacts the world, by changing one decision at a time, and we can change the world. Once enough people start believing this way, we turn self change into global change.*
- *We are here to learn and grow, and to keep expanding our mind and consciousness. Time and energy are too precious to waste; much of them on things that are not making the world a better place.*
- *The only constant in life is change. We must be the change if we wish to see in the world.*
- *Don't judge someone until you've walked in their shoes. Everyone has a story, care enough to listen.*
- *We've been condition from birth. Experience life for yourself and make up your own mind about what is true.*
- *Personal success is the embodiment of a generous, compassionate heart and creative mind. Life is at its best when one whole-heartedly and unconditionally serves the higher good for all.*
- *Awareness is the single most important thing we can cultivate in ourselves and others to improve the world. Higher awareness increases our ability to make every decision in accordance with our deepest values, which I believe are universal values.*
- *Expand your mind to the limits you don't know were possible. Break those limits.*
- *Anything is possible one step at a time.*
- *Now is the time, we are the ones, we have been waiting for.*
- *Life is to be lived! The only greater happiness than knowing you've fully lived your life is knowing that you've helped others achieve the same.*
- *Life is a blessing, and every moment is a choice. Let Spirit lead, live life consciously, and serve.*
- *If you turn on the Light in your home; doesn't the darkness go away? Keep the light on within your soul to keep the darkness away. Please turn on the Light and keep it on! (Quoted by Jeffery Q. Christensen, 2007).*

NOTES

I want to thank you for our journey together and hope these techniques are as helpful to you as they were for me. Certain things are infinite. Magic is one of them, it belongs to no one culture or religion, and it is part of the universal wisdom and natural laws. Magic is filled with the most ancient memories that go back to our ancestors, who lived in natural cycles and understood and appreciated the power and energy that we share with the universe. The word magic can stir these memories and feelings even with the most skeptical minds. I've combined my own experiences with my spirit guides to assist you to embark on your own journey of discovery. Most of us go through life without developing the wonderful, natural, abilities that are Divine given gifts inherent in all of us. I hope this book offers you accessible guidance. Just remember to recognize and listen to your own inner voices by altering your awareness to make contact with the spirits of the departed, guides and your angels. Also try to become very aware of your dreams because as I've mentioned, most contact and communication is within dream states. As you receive messages you will be able to heal and help others.

While walking to work one morning I had a sense of someone walking with me. I looked around and saw no-one. A voice whispered in my ear, saying look up I'm up here. Behold there was my angel. Good thoughts raced through my mind such as; what a nice day to take a walk with my angel.

NOTES

REFERENCES

Cheung, Theresa, *(The Element Encyclopedia of 20,000 Dreams,)* Published by Harper Element, 2004.

Dr. Chopra, Deepak, *(Life after Death,) Crown Publishing Group, 2006.*

Illes, Judika, *(The Element Encyclopedia of 5,000 Spells,)* Published by, Harper Element, 2004.

Llewellyn, *(Witches Datebook, annual,)* Published by Llewellyn Worldwide, annually.

Rav Berg, *(Education of a Kabbalist,)* Published by Kabbalah Centre International, Inc., 2000.

Reed, Ellen Cannon, *(The Witches Qabala,)* Published by Red Wheel/Weiser, LLC, 1997.

Three Initiates, *(The Kybalion-Hermetic Philosophy,)* Publishes by The Yogi Publication, 1912.

Walsh, Jean and Stacy, Barbara, *(The Witches Almanac,)* Published by Self Published, 1971

NOTES

Prayer

May you walk hand in hand with Infinite Spirit.

May your Spirit Guides connect closer to you

with guidance, assistance and unconditional

love on your journey through life with

Love, Light and Healing.

www.ingramcontent.com/pod-product-compliance
Lightning Source LLC
Chambersburg PA
CBHW081343230426
43667CB00017B/2707